1989

The publisher gratefully acknowledges the generous support of the Music in America Endowment Fund of the University of California Press Foundation, which was established by a major gift from Sukey and Gil Garcetti, Michael P. Roth, and the Roth Family Foundation.

1989

---

bob dylan didn't have this to sing about

JOSHUA CLOVER

UNIVERSITY OF CALIFORNIA PRESS

BERKELEY LOS ANGELES LONDON

University of California Press, one of the most
distinguished university presses in the United States,
enriches lives around the world by advancing scholarship
in the humanities, social sciences, and natural sciences.
Its activities are supported by the UC Press Foundation
and by philanthropic contributions from individuals and
institutions. For more information, visit www.ucpress.edu.

University of California Press
Berkeley and Los Angeles, California

University of California Press, Ltd.
London, England

Library of Congress Cataloging-in-Publication Data

Clover, Joshua.
    1989 : Bob Dylan didn't have this to sing about / Joshua
Clover.
        p.   cm.
    Includes bibliographical references and index.
    ISBN 978-0-520-25255-4 (cloth : alk. paper)
    1. Popular music—1981–1990—History and criticism.
2. Rap (Music)—History and criticism.   3. Underground
dance music—History and criticism.   4. Grunge music—
History and criticism.   5. Nineteen eighty-nine, A.D.
I. Title.

    ML3470.C597   2009
    781.6409'048—dc22   2009018653

Manufactured in the United States of America

18   17   16   15   14   13   12   11   10   09
10   9   8   7   6   5   4   3   2   1

The paper used in this publication meets the minimum
requirements of ANSI/NISO Z39.48–1992 (R 1997)
(*Permanence of Paper*).

God knows how we got here. And yet it's a great pleasure to live in a century where such great things are happening, provided one can hide away in a small corner so as to watch the Comedy at one's ease.

—NICOLAS POUSSIN
letter to Paul Fréart de Chantelou,
January 17, 1649

contents

PART TWO
"1989" (A SHOUT IN THE STREET)

illustrations

prologue

In 1989, Paris sang "La Marseillaise." The new opera house was consecrated near the site of the Bastille prison, stormed two hundred years before, on July 14, 1789.

The Bicentennial coincided with the G7 Summit, opening in Paris that day. Led by tricolor-draped diva Jessye Norman, the finance ministers from the Group of Seven industrialized nations and the assembled heads of state served as a chorus for the triumphal singing of the revolutionary anthem in the Place de la Bastille, signaling the Bicentennial as an occasion for the whole of the First World. The spectacle of statecraft was orchestrated by Jean-Paul Goude, former artistic director of *Esquire* magazine.[1]

This commemoration would be entirely supplanted in public consciousness before the year's end. The sanguine dénouement of the occupation in Beijing's Tiananmen Square—sensationalized in the Western media in equal proportion to the Chinese state's attempts at media suppression—had already rendered the French Bicentennial artifactual, mere revolution recollected. François Mitterrand's press conference concluding the Summit was dominated by questions about China, and about the Soviet Union. He forecast no major changes.[2] In less than four months, cascading European events would culminate in the opening of the border between East and West Germany and the disintegration of the Iron Curtain. By the end of December, 1989 could lay claim to having been the most geopolitically laden year since at least 1945.

The story of "La Marseillaise," even relegated to the role of an aside, nonetheless bears on the story this book has to tell about music and cultural memory—about culture and the great events of history. Most Americans likely know the song originally from Rick's Café Américain in the movie *Casablanca,* as a rallying cry for a wounded French patriotism during the Occupation.[3] This provides an affect for the song, if not much historical detail. Resistance to tyranny et cetera. The song belongs to the French Revolution; it is one of the signs that together signal "1789." As the Parisian doctor Poumiès de la Siboutie noted in his journal, "Songs were a powerful revolutionary means, the 'Marseillaise' electrified the populace."[4]

"La Marseillaise," less famously, was also the marching song of the Russian Revolution of 1917, to be replaced by "The Internationale," which would become the Soviet Union's national anthem. The latter would in turn serve as a rallying song for the occupying students and workers in Tiananmen Square. As it happens, "The Internationale" was originally a French song— with lyrics set to the melody of "La Marseillaise."

Thus the song proceeds along two historical paths: one a long arc, a linear narrative in which the nascent French Republic is consolidated over two centuries into a beacon of the First World, an industrial power and cultural center; the other, a series of knight's moves from uprising to uprising, changing at every leap. Two routes from 1789 to 1989, each with quite different valences.

It is perhaps only contingent that the modern era's longest and most complex conflict—the division of much of the globe between Soviet-bloc communism and U.S.-style capitalism—is seen to end exactly two hundred years after the French Revolution, the political struggle commonly held to have given birth to modernity itself. What is surely less contingent is how each of these events could be dated decisively enough for such neat histories, which seem to have their own inarguable logic. Thus the numerical coincidences of modernity take on the aspect of a linear narrative. As Francis Fukuyama puts the matter: "The year 1989—the two hundredth anniversary of the French Revolution, and of the ratification of the U.S. Constitution—marked the decisive collapse of communism as a factor in world history."[5]

The French Revolution may have begun on July 14 with the storming of the Bastille; or perhaps it was earlier, with the National Assembly's refusal to disband, its June 20 "Tennis Court Oath." The signal political change—the abolition of monarchy, the birth of the Republic, France's Year Zero—waited until the Fall of 1792. The crucial and contingent events that unfolded in the interim defy enumeration.

Lived history slips away. Of course. It is replaced with images and stories, eventually a single story, a lone reference point: the storming of the Bastille in Paris on July 14, 1789, which the citizens of France celebrate punctually by singing "La Marseillaise." But the song in question did not exist, had not yet been written.

It was not even the first popular song of the Revolution. That would be "Ah! Ça ira" (its refrain apocryphally inspired by the stumbling French of Benjamin Franklin), which begins "Ah! It'll be fine, it'll be fine, it'll be fine—aristocrats to the lamp-posts!" The sentiments of "La Marseillaise" bear a somewhat different legacy through the generations:

Arise, children of the Fatherland,
The day of glory has arrived;
Against us, tyranny's
Bloody standard is raised.[6]

The striking disparity between these two songs' sensibilities must be in some part one of time and situation. Events were moving with an unknown swiftness; history itself couldn't catch its breath. "Ah! Ça ira" is from 1790; "The Chant of the Rhine Army," as "La Marseillaise" was first called, was not composed until 1792. It was brought to Paris by said army; at that moment, with the Revolution at least three years in, it was not clear what would happen next, or what the Revolution even meant.

The song, that is to say, both does and doesn't belong to 1789. It summons affect, image, and event that seem located in that year without actually being from that year. This is saying something more than the truism that songs escape their original contexts and intentions, that messages shift. It puts on display the process by which process vanishes—wherein fluid, uncertain, debatable, and analyzable meanings congeal and flatten, grow finally fixed.

The Long 1989

THIS IS NOT A HISTORY BOOK. How could it be, when history famously ended in the year in which the book is largely set? Perversely, the events that magnetize the present study—the fall of the Berlin Wall and the end of the Cold War, for which the fall is absolute metonymy—are the very events said to have secured the end of history.

That last phrase, with a terminal but convictionless question mark ("The End of History?"), is the title of Francis Fukuyama's essay first published in the *National Interest* in the summer of 1989, wherein is declared "the triumph of the West, of the Western *idea*."[1] If there was any doubt of the answer at that moment, while the Wall still stood and the border remained closed, it would not survive through the bestselling volume that followed, *The End of History and the Last Man*. In this account, the line from the French Revolution to the end of communism is the line from Hegel to Fukuyama himself.[2] Hegel's vision of the Grande Armée's victory at Jena in 1806 as heralding "a new era of the spirit" is realized in 1989's global apotheosis of liberal democracy—after which, per Fukuyama, "we have trouble imagining a world that is radically better than our own, or a future that is not essentially democratic and capitalist."[3]

That history didn't end is by now not worth remarking. There is nonetheless a specter of actuality in Fukuyama's analysis, and it wants reckoning as something more than a straw man. *We have trouble imagining.* The participle

Figure 1. The building of the Berlin Wall, 1962. (Photo Popperfoto/Getty Images)

is everything. For if we understand Fukuyama to have been making the more modest if still tragic claim that 1989 witnessed the end of *historical thought,* that the public imagination of the West had abandoned a conception of ongoing historical process, of alternative arrangements of daily life—then his suggestion is considerably less laughable. If Fukuyama's description is fixed not to historical truth but to a condition of consciousness arising in a new situation, it swiftly reveals itself as worthy of discussion.

Implicit in this is the significance of popular culture: the great marketplace of the public imagination, and indeed the place where market and imagination struggle over consciousness, over what's thought and what's thinkable. "Pop music" is always at least two facts: the cultural artifact of the song and all that it communicates; and its popularity, its having been claimed by enough people to enter into mass culture. A song may communicate historical experience—including the experience of the end of history—in several different ways. But pop's thinking is always also the thought of the audience, the choice of some songs over others, of selecting *this* and not *that* by way of trying to grab hold of the moment: what it means, how it feels.

Looking across the career of the London band Jesus Jones throws into exacting relief one of the great mysteries: how it is that undistinguished figures can, in a given instant, leap beyond the possible and make something entirely true. Recorded in spring of 1990 but not released until 1991, "Right Here, Right Now" is one of the two songs most identified with the Fall of the Wall, at least in the Anglophone West.[4] It is, more or less, perfect. It was as if they had been waiting for the moment all their lives.

That is what the song is about, of course: "I was alive and I waited, waited," sings Mike Edwards, reaching for an exultant, befuddled falsetto. "I was alive and I waited for this." *This* is the events of 1989, the sudden collapse of the global arrangements and antagonisms known as the Cold War. Behind the lead vocal, in the push-pull of instruments and microchips that organizes the musical track, a fanfare swells as it follows the melody into the chorus, the uplift of "Right here, right now, there is no other place I wanna be / right here, right now, watching the world wake up from history." Apparently Edwards and Fukuyama had been reading the same books, though the singer has perhaps dog-eared as well a page of Joyce's *Ulysses*.

It's a compact track, almost exactly the fabled three minutes that define the classic pop song; two brief verses, lots of chorus. The mix of analog and digital sounds is itself a mini-essay on the state of Anglo pop just then, the balance of rock tradition and the insurgent forms of hip-hop and electronic dance musics. Appropriately, the lyric takes the world-historical convulsion not as a general wonderment, but as a specific problem for pop music. "Woman on the radio talks about a revolution," begins the vocal, "but it's already passed her by." The line targets Tracy Chapman, the folk singer whose self-titled debut had reached number one in both the U.S. and U.K. in 1988—and particularly sets its sights on "Talkin' 'bout a Revolution," which encapsulated Chapman's plaintive blend of progressive liberalism and acoustic guitar that would launch eight million discs.[5] The second verse in its entirety aims its charge at Prince's 1987 single "Sign '☮' the Times" and that song's catalog of hints that the end times are near. In "Right Here, Right Now," Prince's social Armageddon, like Chapman's "revolution," is a visionary leap lacking a real occasion, and so disingenuous. "I saw the decade end when it seemed the world could change at the blink of an eye," runs the Jesus Jones report from 1990, "and if anything, then there's your sign—of the times."

That accounts for almost the whole of the song's two verses, but not quite. If

Edwards seemingly hasn't the chutzpah to name names as he fires shots across the bow of political pop, he screws his courage to the sticking place in the only remaining line of the song, the end of the first verse: "Bob Dylan didn't have this to sing about / you know it feels good to be alive." Fanfare, chorus.

It is easy enough to poke fun at the utopian whispers and creeping apocalypticism of the gloomy artistes, and the song doesn't pass the opportunity by. But behind this lies an unspoken question that makes the song finally haunting: What does pop music do when it *does* have this to sing about? Pop music as we understand it: something not much older than the Berlin Wall, something which could be the Soviet Union's granddaughter. Having turned its 200-second attentions on a fairly regular basis to politics, to social change, to *revolution,* what does pop music do when confronted with an overwhelming surfeit of same? The song has no certain answer. It is discomfittingly ambivalent. Is it anticommunist? Maybe. It has no time for cultural liberalism: *take that, you hipsters who came before! You who whistled in the wind tunnel when it was just a test, when the times they weren't a-changin'. Those weren't beautiful epics, they were just . . . pop songs!* And yet it is the absolute victory of the liberal idea that the song is trying to register. It too is a pop song. It has only timing on its side. The idea must be that pop itself—not Mike Edwards, not Bob Dylan—had been waiting for this moment in order to realize itself, waiting for the conditions when pop could be not righteous but true. And it need say nothing, nothing but that this is the moment, *right here, right now,* in which the uncontainable excess of history itself flashes up and vanishes. "Watching the world wake up—" sings Edwards at the very end, stopping the line short so that *from history* precipitates out, all of us having woken up into something else entirely.

STRUCTURES OF FEELING

And it was something else. Misrecognition scene though it may be, Fukuyama's proclamation means nonetheless to register an irruption of international shifts the truth of which can't be conjured away. In 1989, describing a set of policy prescriptions for countries in fiscal crisis, economist John Williamson coined his fateful phrase: the "Washington Consensus." The term resonated beyond the humming offices of the International Monetary Fund and the World Bank insofar as it could stand not just for a policy line but for what increasingly appeared a world situation: the United States' reign as a "unipolar power," unvexed even symbolically.[6] If this reign would last only a dozen years, a brief and strife-filled new Pax Americana, the period still plays a vital role in narrating Western history. From the perspective of the United States, it constitutes a political belle époque that seemed to reverse the country's decline as global hegemon—a descent that starts around 1973 with the final end of the postwar economic boom and the great image-defeat of the Vietnam War.

For the dissolving Soviet bloc, the changes of 1989 were local phenomena before they were geopolitics. The litany of events from that year is by now familiar, from the departure of the last Soviet armored column from Kabul in February to the year-end election of Václav Havel as president of Czechoslovakia, heading their first non-Communist government in forty-one years. Between these, an unbroken series of startling developments, of which two stand forth. The student occupation of Tiananmen Square begins in April and ends in massacre in June. On November 9, audiences worldwide watch images of Eastern Bloc citizens flowing through the suddenly opened border. Shortly after that, even more resonant images of the Wall's destruction—by hand, by pickaxe, and finally by heavy machinery—begin to beam around the globe. These are just the leading instances of disaster and triumph. Not for nothing does Fukuyama title one of his chapters "The Worldwide Liberal Revolution."[7]

These events all belong to 1989, the category—and just as well to "1989," the concept. One, a container into which can be tossed songs and images and newspaper articles and punctual happenings, anything with a date on it (though as we have already seen, even singularly dated objects can have long and varied provenances, and dates moreover are not always to be trusted). And the other, a shorthand for *what happened,* for the experiential dimension of a capacious swath of history: an index that becomes more impacted, more challenging to unpack, with each passing year.

This book, equally, has two parts, category and concept. The first concerns music; this is a music book before anything else. With some notable exceptions, the music in question is "global, yet American," exactly because the date in question is the moment of America's accession to its role as unchallenged world power. In particular, the book considers genre changes within Anglophone pop music in and around 1989. The accounting of these shifts, which occupies the four chapters of Part One, is largely a descriptive matter, considering some exemplary songs and records that fall along these trajectories of change: songs that can stand as last year's models and next big things, in the industrial clichés.

Raymond Williams's conception of "structures of feeling" likely gets at the situation more precisely: his triad of dominant, residual, and emergent maps elegantly onto culture at various scalar levels, from the breadth of pop music to the vicissitudes of a single subgenre.[8] In these terms, Part One is about emergence in pop music. Specifically, this book begins with a curiosity over an exceptional surplus of emergence from about 1988 to 1991, focused on the *annus mutationis* of the title. Williams's dynamic is always in progress; the occasion of this argument is the way the balance tilted in a certain loaded moment, leaving us with a period characterized by an *emergence of emergence.*

Having said this, there is also something that skips away in Williams's dynamic, increasingly so as a moment under consideration retreats into the past. Moments of emergence are interstices when an old dominant is losing its power to magnetize the field, when formal and social possibilities—even in the overdetermined zones of massively profitable markets—are just a bit more up for grabs than usual. Inevitably, they are likely to host any number of one-offs, nonce styles, goofs, and odd bids at the main chance: curios that sneak in past the doorkeepers in the confusion. One of these will turn out to be the dominant, and will be retrospectively recognized as having been *the* emergent style. Every genre enters the popular imagination as a novelty song that is later seen to be a manifesto, a discourse on new form. Consider how strange "Rapper's Delight" once seemed—or "Rock Around the Clock." To turn matters on their head, one might say that there are no novelty songs, only failed genres; this is perhaps to say that there are no insurrections, only failed revolutions.

The other songs, those that do not found genres, will retain only the honor of their idiosyncrasy and a diminishing revenue stream for whoever owns the publishing—but they too want describing, bearing as they do the traces of the possibilities that pool in the fissures of such tectonic shifts.

This book is largely indifferent to the distinction between genres and subgenres, which seems beyond contextual. To paraphrase Max Weinreich on languages and dialects, the difference between a genre and a subgenre is an army and a navy. Moreover, much music is necessarily missing from this book, including some that a reader might reasonably expect to find here: there is no Pink Floyd, despite their having named an entire album *The Wall* (which their lead singer, Roger Waters, would perform in full at the site of the Berlin Wall in 1990). Neither is there the music of Plastic People of the Universe, the band that took its name from Frank Zappa and became the crux of Czech dissident culture that would unfold into Charter 77 and the Velvet Revolution (nor is there any Zappa himself, despite his role as unofficial attaché to Václav Havel's government, and despite the memorial statue of Zappa to be found in Vilnius, Lithuania).[9] The fundamental question concerns how popular music understood the world in this moment, and how it was being used to understand the world—and it is thus the popular music of this moment that concerns us, particularly when it seems to register change in some significant degree.

THE REAL OF HISTORY

This question summons the argument of the book's second part: the possibility that this constellation of changes in pop music around 1989 might be tied to changes in the world at large—that is, might provide ways of thinking about the historical situation of "1989." This is historicization in reverse, one might say, deriving real conditions from "the mental conceptions that flow from them."[10] From the perspective of a history of music, the matter might also be framed as an attempt to use the world situation—social change and spectacle both—as an occasion to periodize the pop music of that time.

There is something counterintuitive about this. Theodor Adorno, one of the twentieth century's great historicizers, suggests that pop music is a poor candidate for bearing historical particularity. "The whole structure of popular music is standardized," Adorno declared in 1941.[11] "A song-hit" (now a charmingly awkward-sounding translation) "must have at least one feature by which it can be distinguished from any other, and yet possess the complete conventionality and triviality of all others." As is well discussed elsewhere, Adorno's contempt for popular music (jazz, most famously) has problematic social implications, particularly along the axes of both class and race. But if these limitations leave Adorno's critique inadequate to the pleasures of popular music, his account of the market conditions that survive in this music as a kind of form is hard to dispute.

Moreover, pop music does not itself aspire much to history or historicity. Contrarily, it hangs quite a bit on the hook of timelessness—on making time disappear for three or four minutes, a brief shelter from the wind of change. Evanescence is near the heart of the pleasure for a million songs.

For all that, one proceeds on the faith that the seeds of time somehow lodge in these abjected artifacts, like otherwise unknowable neutrinos striking chlorine atoms in a subterranean swimming pool, turning a few to argon, in the famous, beautiful experiment. The belief is that pop songs too come out of actual conditions, and bear their imprint.[12]

This is a different matter altogether from proposing that pop music somehow intervenes in history—that it is a site of resistance or even of insight, of new political awareness. Said optimism would require imagining that it retained some autonomy from the determining powers of the economy, or from the organizing power of ideology. Such a belief was already implausible in 1989; more so now. As Fredric Jameson put the matter in 1984 in his influential essay on postmodernism, "Distance in general (including 'critical distance' in particular) has very precisely been abolished in the new space of postmodernism."[13] In 2002, he put things even more succinctly: "Culture has become the economic, and economics has become cultural."[14] In this reasoning he worries the collapse of various spheres into a single congealed mass of social existence dominated by appearance and most famously described by Guy Debord as "the spectacle."

The argument in Part Two is thus not simply about affixing 1989 pop to "1989" the historical idea, in the manner of cultural studies as it is currently practiced in the university; it is an opportunity to wonder over the possibility of such a connection in the first place. That is to say, it is about the possibilities of culture at that moment. It is a meditation on the rather crude but not yet resolved question of whether pop music has much to tell us about what Jameson calls "the Real of History"—and if so, how so? To what, by the late twentieth century, could popular culture testify?

MORE LIKE A POP SONG

Jameson's own theoretical apparatus allows the pursuit of this testimony—in particular the claims made in *The Political Unconscious* and "Postmodernism, or the Cultural Logic of Late Capitalism." He seems to have glimpsed in advance the situation of Fukuyama's phantasmatic vision: "Premonitions of the future, catastrophic or redemptive, have been replaced by senses of the end of this or that (the end of ideology, art, or social class; the 'crisis' of Leninism, social democracy, or the welfare state, etc., etc.): taken together, all of these perhaps constitute what is increasingly called postmodernism."[15] Jameson's failure to foresee claims about "the end of history" may indicate only that some hubris is beyond imagination.

Nonetheless, Fukuyama must be taken seriously, not least because of the purchase his narrative and slogan found in culture at large, the arena where pop becomes pop and circulates. Fukuyama's version is more like a pop song, after all: a formula that seems at once to tell a total story and condense it into a slogan, a logo, an image. Is that not what the perfect chorus is for—in which "the end of history" becomes a hook so catchy and memorable, so improbably pleasing to repeat, that it spins around the globe in a blink? It seems finally a better explanation for the structure of feeling organized by any number of the songs this book measures, songs indexed inextricably to "1989." It's easy enough to believe that the "wind of change" blowing through the song of that title—the most famous pop song of 1989, or rather "1989"— is the last such wind ever, a perfection and culmination. This is a version of what pop music was always trying to convey; perhaps pop had been biding its time until 1989 came along to make sense of its sensibility.

Certainly, Scorpions had been waiting a good while. A perfectly successful concern, they had survived the years with the usual fraternal bickering, substance abuse, personnel changes, and a few international hits (most of them from the 1984 album *Love at First Sting*) since their formation in 1973.[16] As suggested earlier, there is an account of no little interest in which the story of "1989" begins around this moment. Fukuyama tells part of it himself, with his usual focus on the political: "The current crisis of authoritarianism did not begin with Gorbachev's perestroika or the fall of the Berlin Wall. It started over one and a half decades earlier, with the fall of a series of right-wing authoritarian governments in Southern Europe . . . "[17]

Jameson, as it happens, dates postmodernism to around 1973 in his essay, though—working at the crossroads of culture and political economy—his periodizing facts are different. But the grand narrative of 1973 will have to be told elsewhere; only bits and pieces are rifted through the present work. For the moment, suffice to say that after a decade and a half, Scorpions were well positioned to capture what they would call "the magic of the moment." They were from the city of Hanover, in what was the English zone after the Second World War. Lyricist and vocalist Klaus Meine, born in the year of the Berlin Blockade, had long experience writing for the Anglophone global pop audience (might one say "Anglobal"?). The band specialized in keening power ballads, with all the demographic traversal they imply—and they were comfortable, even happy, with clichés like "magic of the moment," that find their best context in the cross-market, transnational pidgin of anglopop.

This pidgin is of course a site of endless compression, homogenization, emulsification of specifics into the sheen of the general—a machine for cliché. But also a machine for slippage, and oddities. It is worth noting the ignored fact that there is no "The" in the band's name. This is only one of the insistent mistakes revolving around the signal song of the events in question; another is the habit of pluralizing the title as "Winds of Change." Apparently, at the moment there was only one wind—this would seem to matter. It rhymes with Fukuyama's account of all changes as part of a single change, a single historical vector leading toward a unified terminus. All news is one news.

Certainly that is the sense of the video for "Wind of Change": all news is one news.

The role of the music video in pop music's imbricated empire around this moment is a profound and puzzling one. Profound because MTV had become in some regard the most crucial venue for pop music; it was inarguably the most powerful marketing instrument. And puzzling for much the same reason, given that the video form requires music to be something in addition to being music—that it pass through a different medium altogether. One can easily see how such a passage could be of use: pictures had been selling pop for generations. But the image's arrival at the absolute core of the pop music market is nonetheless curious.

Many hands have been wrung over this issue, mostly to the effect of bemoaning the allegedly new requirement that bands be visually appealing rather than musically apt. Despite the evident tradition of image-based marketing, this account of a changed circumstance is difficult to resist; there can be no doubt that MTV's ascent shaped marketing plans from Los Angeles to London. This ascent began in earnest in 1983, with the "second launch" and entry into major standard cable markets; it steepened in 1986, when the channel opened itself up to a broader range of music (most markedly along racial lines; before that moment, an obdurate cultural apartheid had obtained) and began engendering exclusive agreements with the major labels.[18] By the end of the decade, the road to number one passed through MTV's studios—and it was there that pop songs did much of their communicating. This must be reckoned with: scarcely a song mentioned in this book did not have a corresponding video clip in some way suggestive, persuasive, or rhetorically loaded.

That said, a more nuanced history of MTV is needed: of its rise, and the proximate causes and effects. It is striking, to work backward, that within just a few years MTV would abandon the video format altogether and willingly relinquish its position as musical kingmaker. In 1992, MTV began airing *The Real World,* the "reality show" that supplied the dominant format for what would swiftly become, in effect, the world's most successful documentary network. Music clips ebbed, eventually vanishing altogether.

Why might it be the case, then, that the visual form of the pop song, *the pop song as image,* should reach its zenith exactly in this historical passage, when pop music was undergoing the upheavals this book considers, before shortly receding? This is a substantial question, but can only be an aside to this book's inquiry into those changes themselves. The correlation is nonetheless suggestive. Specifically, it suggests the possibility of a shared source that exists beyond the genealogy of pop music in and of itself. To state it plainly, this parallel development proposes that MTV's domination of the image was less a *cause* of musical changes (as the purist hand-wringers would have it) than an *effect* of something else entirely, just as the changes in pop music are effects: the outcomes of a historical dynamic that has a great and particular use for the congealed and singular image-event into which all meanings are bound to collapse.

THE WIND OF CHANGE

After a sourceless wave of applause, the Scorpions video starts with a pensive tune whistled over a minor-heavy chord progression. Tanks on Potsdamer Platz in 1953 (presumably suppressing the strike and protest that came to a head on June 17 of that year with dozens of fatalities); a soldier affixing barbed wire to the new wall in the same location, 1961 (perhaps the Brandenburg Gate is behind them). These images, black and white, are intercut with shots of a vast crowd holding flickering lights in the dark, overlaid with a color image of a single hand holding a sparkler. A spotlight scans side to side: rock lightshow or state surveillance? It is, in fact, impossible to discern whether these images spliced into the newsreel footage are from a vigil at the Wall or a Scorpions concert—a confusion that will propagate aggressively throughout the video. As the vocal starts, an image of Klaus Meine is again overlaid with numerous hands holding sparklers; whether we are watching one or more events is unknowable and, we are starting to suspect, irrelevant.

It's an insipid, magnificent song, from the whistling through the bridge and into the last chorus. Why it was a good candidate for its particular task seems clear enough, even beyond the fact that Scorpions are providentially German. Power ballads exist so that one can feel all sensitive and weepy and overwhelmed, as one does in the face of the historical sublime, but at the same time exaggerated, grandiose—feel like you are at once bigger than God and a tiny Zippo in a world on fire. The video indexes the flames of political violence to the flash-spots of Scorpions' stage show to the audience's personal pyrotechnics, all with unhesitating shamelessness. It turns again and again to tie the song to the Fall of the Wall, even as it locates that as an event among others, such as the obligatory Tiananmen Square icon. The band's

Figure 2. A tiny Zippo in a world on fire: Scorpions, "Wind of Change." (Video dir. Wayne Ishan, Mercury Records)

performance at Potsdamer Platz in 1990 would also do the work of securing the song to the Wall, or to the absence of the Wall, or, really, to the instant of the Wall's coming down.

The video itself takes on the force of a single meaning, threads of sound and language and picture braided together to conjure the instant in question, what happened, how it felt. This is part of the double-faced drive of editing, of collage in general, with its tension between dissolving and reproducing the unities of time and space, sounds and images and ideas. In this confrontation between continuity and discontinuity, it is not too much of a generalization to suggest that the pure products of MTV or the Top 40 regularly take one side over the other. In distinction to, for example, modernism and its polemical dissonances, the music video and the pop song tend toward unification, toward this consolidation of meanings. In their construction they resemble, as suggested, the motion summoned up by "the end of history": the imaging of a single way of being, one that offers itself equally to everybody, into which all trajectories empty. The logic of "the end of history" is in some degree the logic of pop itself.

Here we might repurpose another Jamesonian idea, which for him is attendant to narrative: the imagination of a coherent, unified world which suppresses the fundamental contradictions and discontinuities that are always fissuring actual conditions.[19] The sudden collapse of the Iron Curtain is made to summon up abstractions like *freedom,* or *democracy,* or "the triumph of the West, of the Western *idea.*" But it is impossible to ignore the extent to which the Berlin Wall's deconstruction, as captured in photos, broadcasts, videos, news reports, and the rest, provides a concrete image of unification as an achieved condition, of the overcoming of contradiction and discontinuity.[20] It is the disappearance of the edit, the cut. And this too bears an ideological payload, one that arrives even before the more expressly political messages. It is the spectacularization of coherence itself.

That a feeling, or a set of feelings, might have accompanied this image-event is one of this book's wagers. That the music can grasp or answer those feelings is another, and that the feelings are both complex and contradictory is a third. This situation is complicated by the fact that the book considers an array of genres that might be either too narrow (if one believes that highly commercialized pop can express only its own market imperatives) or too broad (if one thinks of genres and subgenres as existing in discrete form in part because they mean to catch hold of at least somewhat discrete cultural sensibilities, rather than taking part in a broad accounting of a world situation).

The individual chapters, moreover, cannot hope to offer comprehensive accounts of their genres, each of which has generated its own library of book-length considerations. The hope is that, taken together, the exemplary songs, episodes, and apparitions that occupy the chapters of Part One will capture something larger than the truths of each—that the emergent pop genres and attendant social formations might finally be coordinated with the same structure of feeling that captures the spirit of the times, a geopolitical structure of feeling. This requires starting with the belief, or at least the suspicion, that these genres can speak—to each other and to their moment.

THE BOURGEOIS AND THE BOULEVARD

Each of the first four chapters makes account of a different pop genre or, in the case of chapter 4, a metagenre. The chapters are in turn joined by brief bridges that render adjacencies between genres, shared codes that underscore the generalization of certain sensibilities.

The first chapter addresses rap and hip-hop. The conventional attunement of these two terms notes that hip-hop is a cultural complex; rapping or emceeing is one of its four elements, along with DJing, b-boying or breaking, and graffiti. While this account has taken on the status of a shibboleth within the culture, both terms have often applied to the musical form in the broader cultural landscape. But it is exactly the relation of music to culture that is at stake here, and the question of whether substantial changes in one can be found without discovering changes in the other. One of the chapter's arguments is that hip-hop's "Golden Age" ends here in a watershed that is equally musicological and cultural, and that these changes determine each other insistently.

Chapter 1 is bracketed by Public Enemy and N.W.A. (along with the solo debut by N.W.A. producer Dr. Dre). Both acts released epochal albums in 1988; strikingly, the albums didn't compete so much as rise in sequence.[21] *It Takes a Nation of Millions to Hold Us Back* initially dominated the field, charting earlier and higher, topping critic polls in 1988. In the end, however, *Straight Outta Compton* and its progeny would effectively shift the balance of hip-hop from East to West Coast, in concert with Los Angeles's arrival as the national stage for the drama of the African-American underclass. This succession offers a holographic fragment able to hold a rough sketch of hip-hop's history.

As the continent tilted, an implausibly pleasing collection of acts rolled across the national stage. Among others, the chapter considers the Beastie Boys' sample-happy *Paul's Boutique* and Digital Underground's single "The Humpty Dance"; the leveraging of Black Power and gangsta styles to forge a new hip-hop feminism by Queen Latifah and Yo-Yo; the indefatigable Biz Markie; and members of the Native Tongues posse. Of these, Markie and Native Tongues De La Soul loom doubly large for their involvement in landmark legal cases concerning sampling, music production, and ownership—major skirmishes in the intellectual property wars and episodes that changed the material possibilities of the genre and as a result redirected its aesthetic and, it is argued, political trajectories. The chapter understands this struggle as a front in a broader culture war coordinated at exactly this moment when the stakes of hip-hop were up for grabs. Amid all this, the chapter lingers over a largely forgotten New York rapper, both for his musical pleasures and for his capacity to act as a sort of cipher for the changes in progress.

THE SECOND SUMMER OF LOVE

Chapters 2 and 3 both concern the emergence of new genres more than stylistic conversion within an existing genre, though it should go without saying that such apparent newness always has a history, and genres are never birthed full-blown from the forehead of some lonely genius or new machine. The relation to origins is substantial, but these chapters don't endeavor to renarrate aesthetic genealogies. For the most part, they address the moments at which these nascent genres precipitated into the public imagination—when their names could be used effectively in casual conversation among music fans without too much confusion, too many blank looks, en route to being calcified as marketing terms.

In some regard this evolution from subcultural code to music store section heading never quite happened in the United States for the music that organizes chapter 2, the least commercially successful among this book's subjects (which is not to say unsuccessful; fistfuls of dollars changed hands, and a million pounds were incinerated on camera). That is among other things a tale of nomenclatural debates, import-export, and an unpredictable proliferation of microgenres around the electronic dance musics that came down from house, techno, and garage and briefly aligned themselves—a nexus known as "acid house" (and for a time marketed in the United States under the catch-all label of "electronica"). Though the sonic DNA is inextricably braided through eighties Chicago, Detroit, and New York, it's the period immediately around 1989 that sees the rise of acid house in the United Kingdom and its corresponding cultural form of the rave, shortly to become a global phenomenon.

Rave is the live term here; in ways similar to *hip-hop,* it wavers, in the moment, between serving as casual designation for a musical style or styles and referring to the culture arrayed around the music—and specifically, to the parties that married one to the other.

These parties are the chapter's sundial. The era could be clocked by songs, from the dawn of, for instance, 1988's "Theme from S'Express," by S'Express, through the late night of the KLF's epic "3 A.M. Eternal (live at the s.s.l.)," rereleased smashingly in 1991. Or it could be mapped by regions, by rave's two geographical foci: London to the south, of the endless scenes and strata; and Manchester to the north, the Luxor of the age with its daft collosi of Stone Roses and Happy Mondays, bestriding Tony Wilson's Factory Records and Haçienda nightclub.

The significations of individual acts are not, however, what is centrally at stake in chapter 2 (much less stylistic development or intercity competition). Rather, it's the emergence, in just this period, of a subculture and a sensibility and even a politics—one formed just as much in scenes lacking recognizable bands or venues, in warehouses and eventually in the mobile raves along London's M25 Orbital Motorway and elsewhere in the U.K. countryside.

These parties were early on known as "Acid House Summers"; it was in 1989 that they were rebranded "rave parties" in the British press. This will be the solstice of the long "Second Summer of Love": a term that, strangely but conveniently, was applied not to a single season but to the full span 1988–1991, as well as to each of the actually existing summers of 1988 and 1989. What might be meant, in summoning the specter of San Francisco's 1967 and of a more generalized and long-bankrupt hippie tradition, is one of the curiosities herein. Why this belated summer lasted so damned long is another.

NEGATIVE CREEP

Chapter 3 also explores the sensibilities of a new genre, in eighties Seattle: grunge, first used as a genre term around 1987–1988, but without a real genesis until the national success of Nirvana. If the rave era is an epic without a hero, grunge bids to be the most successful genre to base itself so thoroughly on a single act: an implausibly messianic upwelling, down to its singular martyrdom.[22] Nirvana released their first single in 1988, and their cultishly received debut album, *Bleach,* in 1989; in January 1992, their album *Nevermind* replaced Michael Jackson at the top of the charts in a completion of what the music industry experienced as an epochal shift. Similarly popular—and in the case of Pearl Jam, more popular—acts followed, though none of them would synthesize mass appeal and critical triumph so utterly. And none would take on anything like Nirvana's mythic aspect, fueled disastrously by Kurt Cobain's suicide in 1994. The genre would swiftly be adulterated into radio's Modern Rock format, even as the anti-fashion of the Seattle counterculture found itself paraded by models on New York runways. By 1994, grunge was little but a lifestyle brand bound to be disavowed by anyone with remaining subcultural affiliations—an episode of pop eating itself at breathtaking velocity.

In retrospect, grunge was arguably the last next big thing in the rock tradition, before market balkanization and the global ascendancy of hip-hop. That this should play out precisely during the period in question is no small matter. Like various rock "revolutions," it was also a reformation, laying sometimes disingenuous claim to a deskilled musical simplicity that is taken as a return to rock 'n' roll's primal nature.[23] Of particular interest is grunge's much-bruited inheritance of the punk rock tradition—a lineage hypostatized in the title of the documentary film *1991: The Year That Punk Broke.* Grunge, that is to say, is imagined to be at once genesis and resurrection: an ambivalent situation, answered by a taste for ambivalence that charges the music itself, as both sonic form and emotional content.

These are dangerous waters to enter: the number of serious, book-length studies of punk rock is ever-growing, and a single chapter can't hope to summarize the material or the endlessly freighted debate around the historical and political import of punk. Our study is inevitably more narrow, concerning itself mainly with the matter of ambivalence—with continuities and ruptures between punk and grunge, and the kinds of social relations figured by these musics.

THE BILLBOARD CONSENSUS

Pop music, largely as a matter of definition, cannot be emergent. If hip-hop, rave, and grunge succeed in standing as both cultural and musical orders, pop does neither. The truth of pop music is neither musicological nor specifically cultural, but economic and after-the-fact: popularity itself, as measured in sales and radio play (measurements that would change dramatically in 1991 with the shift to Nielsen SoundScan tracking). In any week of any year, there is always a Top 40, a Hot 100. Seen through money-colored glasses, pop is always the dominant.

But this is not to say that pop lacks characteristics that reward attention, nor that pop is unable to be a sign of the times. Chapter 4 attempts to take the measure of pop music around 1989, and argues that even if pop can be abjected for its sensation of deracinated timelessness, it paradoxically *had its time* at the end of the Cold War exactly because the sensation of pop captured a dimension of social experience at the end of the Cold War. To put the matter perversely: rather than pop emerging in new history, new history emerged to meet pop.

Some of the music considered in the chapter belongs to mayfly acts recalled finally via a single song, such as Deee-Lite, and period inventions that implausibly survived to even greater success, such as teenpop. Some music belongs to bands with more durable careers that nonetheless found the summits of the pop chart only within the exigencies of this era, as in the case of the Divinyls and Sinéad O'Connor. And then there were those of ongoing success who nonetheless hazarded their finest moments here, such as Madonna and the extraordinary case of George Michael's "Freedom '90," which despite its title went out of its way not to be about global politics.

The chapter's argument doesn't require that these songs have political or historical content. Indeed, almost the opposite: the inquiry regards the extent to which history can sometimes only appear as trace, as mood and affect—the very things pop is more apt to capture than the grain of quotidian life amid great upheavals, or the subtleties and grandeurs of history writ large. Nonetheless, there is room for songs that seem desperate to clutch at history itself, such as the catalogic spasm of Billy Joel's "We Didn't Start the Fire"—lead single from an album released on November 10, 1989. The chapter ends with a consideration of the stirring political anthem from Sweden's Roxette, "Listen to Your Heart," the song that had just hit number one that same week, which is to say that it was ensconced atop the Billboard singles chart on November 9, 1989, when, after twenty-eight years, a partitioned Berlin was thrown open: the Fall of the Wall.

ONE

The Fall of the Wall—that's a phrase to conjure with. The Wall itself was a kind of conjuration, summoned as if overnight to secure both pragmatic and representational goals. The concrete icon grew to be the densest object in the world, compressed as it was by the weight of two world empires pressing against it without surcease.

The Fall of the Wall, as an image-event that must be constantly recalled, is no less an icon; it replaced the Wall itself with a rapidity no less startling than the speed with which one story about the world situation replaced another. As an image-event, the Fall doesn't validate Fukuyama's account so much as render its contours visible. A city with a wall removed. History with the history removed. And still this iconic absence, *the Fall of the Wall,* lingers in Potsdamer Platz and Checkpoint Charlie, below the Brandenburg Gate and in the metro's reopened "ghost stations." This persistence of vision wherein *the absence of a singular image,* that of the Wall, becomes itself a singular image explaining everything—this is the representational truth of the end of history, a message that presents itself as universal and as easily understandable as a pop song.

So then: did history end in pop music too? Did that story get told, that structure of feeling captured, in the Hot 100, in the clubs and warehouses and radios of the first world? This is the possibility taken up in Part Two. At least part of that sensation, a deflated paralysis in the face of history itself, is found in "Right Here, Right Now," to which Part Two returns in order to begin its orchestration into a single account of the emergences and apotheoses of the preceding chapters.

Certainly the changes tracked in the first four chapters have their own cultural coordinates, each worthy of its own detailed accounting. Nonetheless, they can also be attuned toward a decisively coherent understanding, a pop worldview, which echoes, and even reproduces, the basic logic of the moment. This in turn begins to suggest pop's capacity for grasping, as a mode of cultural thought, world-historical events often thought to be beyond it.

However, this analytic path runs up against one of the horizons of the story: the plausibility of suggesting that the world events of "1989" have a single logic, that there is one story that can make sense of the details. This would be to settle for Fukuyama's version, in the end, mirroring the progressive historical teleologies that end in a single, triumphal truth. From a different perspective, this isn't the truth but the problem. Here we recall, to focus only on the most freighted example, that the brutal events that unfolded beneath the Gate of Heavenly Peace in that year are related only obliquely to the story of the Wall and the end of the Cold War.

The year 1989, we must concede without hesitation, had not one but two poles of world-historical force. The Tiananmen Square massacre is by some measure even more shocking than the events of Berlin, given the death toll, governmental cover-up, and brutal revisions of history. Certainly these two moments share some qualities and some geopolitical backstory as episodes in the unwinding of twentieth-century Communist seizures of state power. From that point, however, the two events diverge extraordinarily, and in some regard might be seen to have *opposite* dynamics—a point that will be touched upon later. For the moment, what bears notice is the extraordinary success of the Western narrative of liberal democracy at capturing the meaning of Tiananmen Square for itself as a pungent but, in the last summary, secondary instance of the Fall of the Wall. In the realm of actual events, this is perhaps the most violent of all elisions, conducted with breathtaking casualness; consider the inclusion of images from Beijing in the "Wind of Change" video, at once index to and agent of the ongoing collapse of meanings to a single point. That this book attunes its analysis to the Fall of the Wall is not to suggest that that image-event deserves its position, alone astride the summit of contemporary history. Rather, it means to wonder over the vanishing process that allows such a consolidation—that indeed requires it—and to understand pop as participating in that process, even as it struggles to register what is amiss within it.

The unified and uncontested account is itself a kind of end of history—the thinning of historicity into a single idea, the image-event in the form of an idea. What does the popular meaning of "1989" offer, after all, if not unity and coherence?

The concluding motions of Part Two look to the discontinuities of Fuku-yama's account, and pop's relation to it. To do so it returns to the musics of the first four chapters, returns more than once, considering them from different vantages. How can pop music register an end to history when it hasn't ended? Does it capture discontinuity, contradiction, depth? Is there much to say beyond the well-worn suggestion that mass culture is a machine for ideological reproduction, singing back to us messages of convenience in the guise of social truths?

Here some of Jameson's propositions are of considerable use. If pop music did indeed develop, around 1989, "senses of the end of this or that," it would seem to follow Jameson's description of the postmodern. His most aggressive political indication is that "this whole global, yet American, postmodern culture is the internal and superstructural expression of a whole new wave of American military and economic domination throughout the world"—that the ungraspable totality of American power defies the effort to tell its story and is thus a different sort of narrative failure than Fukuyama's victorious *exeunt omnes*.[24] However, this book's final movement concerns an adjacent idea: that pop has in this moment grasped, within its brutal and jubilant reductions and excesses, exactly what's missing from the picture called the end of history—that pop preserves within its blind spot the kernel of his-torical truth, of actual discontinuities, of the dynamics and processes that have not in fact come to an end. Thus, in the final accounting, pop has an ambiguous—even dialectical—relation to historical knowledge and to the world wherein, per the Retort collective, "American victory in the Cold War was rendered in retrospect magical, unanalyzable, by the mantra 'The Fall of the Wall.'"[25]

WHAT COMES AROUND GOES AROUND

This book was finished in 2009, eight years into the current American era, which follows on the political belle époque of 1989–2001. It is worth nam-ing something of the strangeness of its bracketing conflicts, the Cold War and the "war on terror." Both in their own ways are metawars—even, by one logic, postmodern wars. This is not to say that they are fragmentary (though they are); that they often appear depthless, an endless series of surface effects (though they do); or that they are endlessly projected "mediatic" events, as Régis Debray would put it (though they are this as well). What is at stake is the extent to which, in these cases, the political, economic, religious, juridical, and cultural spheres seem to have collapsed into a self-same, eccentric orbit of deterritorialized conflict, of which each local hot war can't quite manage to be an instance. And so it is that, for example, cultural Islam finds itself part of a war zone that is no less real for being an ideological phantasm.

One of the ironies of this book is that it begins with a foot in both wars: in the late hours of the Cold War, but also in cultural Islam as it was most visible in America at that time. A current within hip-hop from its earliest days, the teachings of the Nation of Islam and the Nation of Gods and Earths had achieved, by the late eighties, a motive force within hip-hop's ascending profile—militant forms of an Afrocentric commitment that had blossomed into the heart of the genre's cultural politics.

PART ONE

1989

(the unconfined unreckoned year)

CHAPTER 1

The Bourgeois and the Boulevard

"1989! THE NUMBER, ANOTHER SUMMER!" So begins Public Enemy's "Fight The Power," opening the soundtrack to the Spike Lee film *Do the Right Thing*. The charged and confrontational movie opened on June 30, 1989, amid a maelstrom of controversy—in part for its ending with a Brooklyn race riot triggered by the film's protagonist Mookie, played by Lee himself.

Public Enemy was, in that moment, at the height of its powers. The year before, the group had released what was then the most influential album in hip-hop's history: *It Takes a Nation of Millions to Hold Us Back*. The densely layered, discomfiting sounds of the Bomb Squad production team (led by Hank Shocklee) and leader Chuck D's mercurial verbal militancy seemed like the zenith of hip-hop's Black Power and Black Nationalist movement, which had been for several years ascendant.[1]

The moment contained just the same the seeds of its own annihilation. On the first day of July, following a month of remarkable controversy, the headline "Public Enemy Ousts Member over Remarks" made the front page of leading trade journal *Billboard*.[2] Professor Griff (Richard Griffin) had been the band's road manager and served as head of the S1Ws, "Security of the First World," a cadre who minded the stage during shows clad in military apparel clearly appropriated from the Fruit of Islam, the paramilitary defense force of the Nation of Islam. It was in Griff's role as the group's Minister

Figure 3. Black Power anthem: Public Enemy and the Security of the First World. (DVD "It Takes a Nation: London Invasion 1987," MVD Visual)

of Information, however, that he stated—during a May interview for Sun-Myung Moon's notoriously conservative *Washington Times*—that Jews were responsible for "the majority of wickedness that goes on across the globe."[3] This was not the extent of his offensive commentary, the brunt of which was anti-Semitic as well as homophobic and which endeavored to cite Henry Ford's *The International Jew*. At the June 21 press conference announcing Griff's dismissal, Public Enemy's leader Chuck D insisted, "We are not anti-Jewish, we are not anti-anybody—we are pro-black, pro-black culture, pro-human race. . . . You can't talk about attacking racism and be racist."[4]

Four days after the press conference, a small-scale riot broke out when Chuck announced from the stage in Philadelphia that this was to be their last show. This would have been an extraordinary claim in any circumstance, given Public Enemy's stature at the time: the foremost hip-hop act in the United States, and thus the world. They would re-form shortly, but the sequence of events signaled the beginning of the end for their preeminence within the genre, and for the genre itself in its then-current form.

Largely forgotten is that Public Enemy shared the bill that night in Philadelphia with N.W.A. (Niggaz With Attitude). The latter band had released their own epochal album on January 25, 1989: *Straight Outta Compton*. While scarcely lacking in conflict, the collection, first circulated in 1988, was entirely absent the programmatic commitments of Public Enemy and their *compañeros* in Black Power and Black Nationalist hip-hop; recorded for less than $10,000, it would shortly match *Nation of Millions* in platinum sales. It's worth recalling that, while increasingly ambitious historians trace rap to the dawn of the seventies and before, 1989 was the first year that the Grammies awarded a prize to the genre, then only three years from its first number one album.

The Spectrum show was thus a chiasmus in the genre's history. By year's end, N.W.A. would replace Public Enemy as hip-hop's cause célèbre. The Griff episode would be early in a swift series of sometimes calamitous events, culminating in the riots at the acquittal of the police officers accused of beating Rodney King and the release of N.W.A. producer Dr. Dre's solo album, *The Chronic*—a sequence that would shift the genre's celestial mechanics and cultural imaginary to Los Angeles, eclipsing New York entirely.

But this shift was not simply one of industrial geography, comparable to rock-centered pop music's move from New York to the rising media capital of Los Angeles in the late sixties and early seventies. It also took part in a rejiggering of the popular representation of Black youth and the Black underclass in general, one with substantive problematic social implications and lineages.

This is the emergence traced in this chapter: not of a new genre, but of a change within a genre so substantial, with such cultural force, that it feels more unsettling than the simply new—as if the earth had suddenly reversed the direction of its spin. The shift can be glossed as that from the style of *Nation of Millions* to the style of *Straight Outta Compton;* or of East Coast to West Coast; or from soul samples typified by James Brown to funk beats exemplified by Parliament-Funkadelic. In such topsy-turvy moments, as one set of formal habits shatters and another begins to condense, a frontier feeling comes; the period is, among other things, an era of chaotic, dead-end stylistic inventiveness most familiar from the birth of genres.

Still, it would not do justice to the situation to equate the emergence in question entirely with style or geography. It takes place at the moment when hip-hop is under attack on numerous fronts: aesthetic, cultural, legal. The terms of the change from Public Enemy to N.W.A. are just as much thematic, social, political; it is equally a leap from Black Power and Black Nationalist hip-hop to gangsta rap. That is to say, the conversion is a matter of styles and worldviews at once. It is a formal and ideological tandem which haunts this book; they change together or not at all. This chapter is concerned not with naming the change so much as understanding its particulars—in grasping the fires of the moment and the forces that helped reshape a genre in the era's crucible.

THINKIN' OF A MASTER PLAN

Harry Allen, journalist and one-time "Media Assassin" for Public Enemy, referred to Islam as "hip-hop's unofficial religion"—though not one which is unified. Multiple and sometimes-competing Muslim sects and faiths played a role in hip-hop's rise. Increasingly this influence has tended toward the older tradition of Sunni Islam; in its earlier period, hip-hop was more identified with modern, United States–based teachings (a history inseparable from the oft-overlooked fact that as of 1992, according to the American Muslim Council, the largest demographic component of Islam in the United States was African-American: 42 percent.)[5]

By the end of the eighties, hip-hop was strongly identified with the Nation of Islam (NOI), under the leadership of Louis Farrakhan. The Nation was founded in 1930 by Wallace Fard Muhammad in Detroit, drawing early membership (including future leader Elijah Muhammad) in part from unemployed autoworkers—an irony, given Henry Ford's views on race and religion. Their teachings would be interpreted and disseminated most famously by Malcolm X, ambivalent martyr of Black militancy and post-Bandung Pan-Africanism, who before his death completed the shift from the Nation to Sunni Islam. The shift was echoed structurally when, at the time of Elijah Muhammad's 1975 death, NOI moved closer to traditional Sunni Islam and changed its name to the Muslim American Society. This in turn made way for Farrakhan's refounding of the Nation—an occurrence almost exactly contemporaneous with the appearance of rap's first national hit in 1979.

However, rap had a parallel and longer-standing affiliation, through Afrika Bambaataa's Zulu Nation, with the Nation of Gods and Earths (most often known as the Five Percent Nation, or Five Percenters). This breakaway sect was begun by Clarence 13X, who had attended Malcolm X's Nation of Islam temple in Harlem before departing in 1963. "The focus of the 5 Percenters' belief system includes numerology, cryptic scientific theory, and a more extreme race theory. In this theology, 85 percent of the masses are ignorant, 10 percent are 'bloodsuckers of the poor,' and only 5 percent know the truth."[6] These 5 percent are "gods" descended from the original "Asiatic Black man":

each Allah, each obligated to be a "poor righteous teacher," eloquent and committed to the transmission of sacred knowledge. Similarly, the Five Percent doctrines of the Supreme Mathematics and Supreme Alphabet provide ready content and hermetic shelter for the marginalized; significantly, they also authorize measures of lyrical formalism while suggesting that formal systems such as numerology themselves have content. One can see the appeal of this formation for a rhetorician.

The emphasis on teaching, and on verbal formalism as a pedagogical tool—mnemonics, acronyms, anaphoric theses—is shared with Nation of Islam, and numerous emcees have shifted fluidly between the beliefs of the two sects, sometimes as matters of lyrical convenience, other times in synthesizing a vision for themselves and their audience. The power of preaching and teaching, of divine and secular knowledge, in turn figures as the foundation for a program of self-empowerment.

Of tantamount importance, the project of Black self-empowerment aligns the teachings of both the Five Percenters and the Nation of Islam with rap's early development as an art form. The material, technological conditions allowing for rap's genesis were orchestrated by the use of consumer electronics (most famously the turntable) as tools for the production, rather than reproduction, of music. This development is of course inseparable from rap's struggle to be recognized as a legitimate music. Such a sequence—new art made by non-professionalized performers, followed by a backlash that pretends to police not the social eruption but the terms of the aesthetic—is not a new story. In this case, the backlash has been as extended and contentious as it is racialized. Such a conflict can only be understood as an attempt to maintain the barriers of entry which this new material empowerment had battered down, effectively allowing artists from a previously excluded class and race position to produce material for mass culture (albeit still mediated by certain studio and radio demands). New form, new social access, new content.

Thus it was inevitable that the content of hip-hop would swiftly come to express the possibility, novelty, and force of such self-empowerment, and so gather in the self-empowerment discourses circulating in the hip-hop and broader Black community. These discourses would equally mutate rap's artistic structures in a way that encapsulates the dialectical development of ideology and aesthetic form—a development most apparent in formidably talented emcee Rakim (Rakim Allah, born William Michael Griffin, Jr.), who effectively reimagined the lyrical possibilities of rap on his first two albums with Eric B, *Paid in Full* and *Follow the Leader* (1987 and 1988, respectively). Stretching enjambed sentences across syncopated and densely rhymed lines, Rakim did for rap something on the order of what Bob Dylan had done for rock and roll. Beyond technical triumph, Rakim fashioned a new rhetorical machine, able to articulate extended ideas as persuasively as catchphrases. He was pleased to use both, to connect old-school hustles about moving the crowd with doctrinal rallying cries in a style that instantly rendered obsolete the end-stopped couplet and quatrain format of early rap:

> From century to century you'll remember me
> In history, not a mystery or a memory—
> God by nature, mind raised in Asia,
> Since you was tricked, I have to raise ya
> From the cradle to the grave,
> But remember you're not a slave
> Cause we was put here to be much more than that
> But we couldn't see it because our mind was trapped
> But I'm here to break away the chains, take away the pains
> Remake the brains, reveal my name

Rakim's formal revolution was thus also a revolution of ideas, or of the potential for ideas. The effect was to identify rap's cultural power and Black Power explicitly, and to do so with a particular understanding: that the rhetoric of Black self-empowerment, now indistinguishable from eighties hip-hop, was not a bootstrapping self-determination but an oppositional stance, a Black nationalism based on a racialized theology.

FARRAKHAN'S A PROPHET AND I THINK YOU OUGHT TO LISTEN

Numerous Five Percenter– and Nation of Islam–influenced emcees circulated through hip-hop in the eighties and after.[7] What bears most directly on our story is not so much that such figures existed, or that they played a role in hip-hop's development, but rather their increasing salience over the second half of the decade—the fact that there was a desire, a market, for such representations and polemics. This desire was by any measure encompassing. By the end of the eighties, hip-hop style *meant* Afrocentric commitments, fashions, and rhetoric—and crucially, this style was neither apolitical nor vacantly "positive" but embraced a consciously confrontational politics. Public Enemy was both producer and product of this sea change, more intimately bound up in its workings than any of its cohort. The group's intensity approached the millenarian: "Countdown to Armageddon, '88 you wait." By 1989, Chuck could claim with considerable authority, "Public Enemy is the official voice of the rap world, Black youth, oppressed youth and yes, many white youth in the western world."[8] At the end of the year, leading pop music critic Robert Christgau saw the group as almost pure cause, and was specific about the effects wrought: "they have actually instigated a species of leftish Afrocentrism among kids who three years ago thought gold chains were dope."[9]

Public Enemy achieved this reputation in part because of its insistence on articulating the new politics *as a historical development*—as a supersession of rap's early ethos, that of partying and self-celebrating proclamations (self-empowerment as contentless desire, one might say). This supersession preserved the earlier tradition within itself, even while turning it upside down. The best-known example is the inversion of a Beastie Boys title from 1986, "(You Gotta) Fight for Your Right (to Party!)," which returns as *Nation of Millions'* closing track, "Party for Your Right to Fight." "Bring the Noise" at once celebrates Run-DMC's formative role in the genre ("Run-DMC first said a deejay could be a band") and announces why their spirit is no longer adequate to the situation. This is again achieved through inversion of source lyrics: "Never badder than bad 'cause the brother is madder than mad."[10]

Inversion is a suggestive effect, as if the restructuring of the tradition toward anger and conflict was a way of setting hip-hop on its feet so as to address actual conditions. This political mode of confrontation is not identical to Black Nationalist aspirations but is consistently aligned with them. The same song from *Nation of Millions* hazards the cry of what should rightly follow rap's formative "Old School" years: "Farrakhan's a prophet and I think you ought to listen to / what he can say to you, what you ought to do."

Such progressions, keeping faith with rap's roots while growing toward the most radical social engagements, made Public Enemy both the figures and figureheads par excellence for hip-hop's political turn, as did the group's deftness at addressing overlapping but varied audiences. This was achieved in part by the interplay of Chuck's role as a prophet of rage and the more wayward, everyman charms of sideman Flavor Flav; and in part by the insistent scale-jumping from street scene to allegorical narrative to historical lesson and systemic analysis, all of which allowed the group, in one of its best-known passages, to "rock the hard jams, treat it like a seminar / reach the bourgeois, and rock the boulevard."[11]

The couplet marks the time. It offers two pairs, and insists on the necessity of both: aesthetic success must accompany political content as a pedagogical necessity, and communication must cross lines of class, race, and geography to exceed subcultural status. This double synthesis, then, is the program for a political art. This is the measure of Public Enemy's achievement, rather than articulacy or militancy as such. That is, their significance lies in their realization of an explicitly social-political, confrontational problematic in relation to an aesthetic form that expressed the same problematic otherwise: a total work that solicits engagements and generates affects in multiple ways.

Neither *realization* nor *total* here is meant to indicate a perfectly coherent program, much less a triumphal artificing of an ideological position. If the group was one day making nationalist demands, on another they were taking aim at economic structures while distancing themselves from the Nation's theological strain—as in Chuck's 1989 assertion, "I follow the Nation because Minister Farrakhan and the Nation show us economic self-sufficiency in America and that's my sole use for this information."[12]

BLACK STEEL IN THE HOUR OF CHAOS

In 1988 and 1989, at its zenith, Public Enemy is marked by an incoherence that is both accurate to the situation of confrontation and keeps faith with the politics' necessary undigestibility. The Bomb Squad's sonic collage, built up sometimes from dozens and dozens of samples in a given song spliced into an immersive soundscape, sets a tension between rupture and continuity which serves to "suggest affirmative ways in which profound social dislocation and rupture can be managed and perhaps contested in the cultural arena."[13] The effect, however, is neither consistently affirmative nor alien to the literal. The Bomb Squad sound generally has a leading edge: something shifting around the tones of an alarm or police siren, the promise of imminent violence, meant to produce the state of unrelieved pressure driving the listener "to the edge of panic," as one song puts matters.

The sound is one of the decisive inventions of the century's music. Theodor Adorno claims that an artwork must "integrate thematic strata and details into [its] immanent law of form and in this integration at the same time maintain what resists it and the fissures that occur in the process of integration."[14] As Daniel Thomas-Glass has argued, this is exactly the form of the Bomb Squad's confrontational sound: "So an artwork must build itself of the antagonisms that are necessarily present in the administered world . . . while at the same time resisting the urge to present these problems in the form of a coherent whole. Adorno's phrase for what this success looks (or sounds) like is dissonance."[15]

Along with preserving the antagonism that is the social foundation of Public Enemy (and, we would argue, the entire genre's foundation in the late eighties), this dissonance allows the sound to serve multiple functions. It gives the listener the affective experience of constant pressure, surveillance, and threat of violence, which are horizons of daily life in communities of the Black underclass. For this purported core audience of hip-hop, the sound is a strange version of the familiar, a way of grasping the existential truth of a shared experience. For an audience increasingly comprising more and less affluent white youth, however, the sound arrives as an aesthetic attack more difficult to naturalize or distance than narrative: a largely alien experience that refuses to offer itself as a pleasure. At the same time, the sound's rebarbative edge is explicitly figured as a weapon, as "black steel" turned back on the armed structures of domination for which the police are both agents and synecdoche.

Less allegorically, the Bomb Squad sound turns the tables of cultural attack. Rather than trying to establish the form's musicality in refutation of the persistent critique of the genre, it takes up the terms confrontationally. *You think rap is just sound and fury? I'll give you sound! I'll give you fury!* Hank Shocklee, Bomb Squad leader, accounts this antimusicality a conscious decision: "We didn't want to use anything we considered traditional R&B stuff—bass lines and melodies and chord structures and things of that nature."[16]

But in accepting the terms, it refutes them just the same, conceiving black noise as a countermusicality bearing the same predicates: communicative, formally persuasive, emotionally charged. The Bomb Squad's noise bears a particular experience of everyday life, for which no relief is proposed; instead we have a counterattack of equivalent fury, equally systemic—a defensive assault in both sound and lyric. As Chuck wrote in an unreleased statement during the Griff crisis, "Black Power is only a self-defense movement that counterattacks the system of white world supremacy, not white people or the religious sects they choose. It does not mean anti-white, it means anti-a-system that has been designed by the European elite."[17] This goes for the sound as well as the politics. And this is what comes to a peak, and a shockingly sudden decay, at the time of "Fight the Power" in the summer of 1989.

The collapse of the Black Nationalist project can be deciphered in Public Enemy's first new song after the summer. "Welcome to the Terrordome" was the lead single in advance of *Fear of a Black Planet,* P.E.'s 1990 album; released in late 1989, the track fractures dramatically in the face of crisis. The song preserves the structure of confrontation, from its gladiatorial title (it served as entrance music for World Heavyweight Champion Mike Tyson) and nerve-jangling musical bed, through its lyrics. But the valences of confrontation shift and spasm like a high-pressure garden hose snaking from one's hands. The rap includes seemingly anti-Semitic lyrics that inevitably set off a further cultural conflagration, by now spinning through international news media.[18] In other moments, the song's furies alight in surprising places:

> Every brother ain't a brother
> Cause a black hand
> Squeezed on Malcolm X the man
> The shootin' of Huey Newton
> From a hand of a Nigger pulled the trigger

Beyond the increasingly habitual martyrology, the move to call out the Black community (this is not the song's only passage to do so) is at once shocking and historically eloquent, for it succeeds in forecasting exactly hip-hop's turn at the end of the Golden Age. This turn, the terms of the emergence organizing this chapter, can now be described in more structural terms than simply naming the shift in style, sound, or geography. The shift from Black Power and Black Nationalist to gangsta rap, in and around the year 1989, is a radical revision of the mode of social relations organizing the imaginative space of Black culture. It can be rendered schematically as the turn from inter-group confrontation to intra-group conflict: the *emergence of the internalization of struggle*.

AS NASTY AS THEY WANNA BE

The period we have been puzzling over is exactly what is generally agreed to be the "Golden Age of hip-hop" (a span generally understood to last from around 1986 through 1989). One might limn this period as beginning with Run-DMC's *Raising Hell* and "La-Di-Da-Di" by Doug E. Fresh and Slick Rick, as is often proposed.

It is perhaps more schematically understood as reaching from the success of the Beastie Boys' *Licensed to Ill* to the failure of Black Power hip-hop (that is, from the predictable irony of a white act achieving rap's first number one album, through the ascent of Black Power and Black Nationalist hip-hop, to the bitter reversal of Griff's anti-Semitic remarks and the concurrent crisis).

That is to say, the genre's high era is continuous with the rise of Black Power and Black Nationalism; the Golden Age of hip-hop is none other than the age of political confrontation along race and class lines. This is a truth that wants reckoning.

It cannot be surprising that hip-hop would be confronted in return at the moment of its greatest popular militancy. This took place on multiple fronts, and in some degree had internal causes. Griff's comments are at once expressions of actual, indefensible beliefs and symptoms of a political rhetoric reaching its own horizon, compelled to reach after increasingly incendiary claims to maintain its claim on radicality in the face of its own success.

Nonetheless, the attacks on hip-hop at this moment are so hydra-headed that the Griff episode, without denying it its scandalous particularity, seems to belong to the overdetermination of causes that lowered the curtain on hip-hop's Golden Age. What becomes clear is the way in which the counterrevolution not only shattered the exhausted primacy of Black Power and Black Nationalist hip-hop, but also produced the specific conversion to gangsta rap.

The counterrevolution can be divided into the three overlapping fronts: the aesthetic, intensifying the ongoing popular rejection of rap as a legitimate art form; the legal, both in obscenity trials and, most decisively, in the intellectual property battles that sought to criminalize the very method of the music's production; and the cultural, which is to say the "culture war" that devoted considerable effort to decrying rap's pernicious influence on public morals and the social fabric.[19]

In 1990, L. L. Cool J was the first rapper featured on acoustic-styled "MTV Unplugged"; his show featured a full band and, though much celebrated at the time, was a craven capitulation. Around this time, the "acid jazz" style of live-band hip-hop, begun in the U.K. around 1987, found some popularity in the United States. Rap acts, meanwhile, began sampling heavily from jazz styles, as well as recording and performing increasingly with live (frequently jazz) instrumentation. All of these developments served to signify a more traditionally accomplished musicality, and met with decidedly mixed success both in deflecting *besserwisser* bourgeois critique and in producing interesting records.

What increasingly revealed itself as an identical conflict was played out in the courts: "The sudden interest in sampling and copyright laws . . . happens to be focused on rap, a musical style which is largely dependent on sampling techniques."[20] The "sudden" timing was conspicuous: the precedent-setting cases were launched starting in 1989 and largely concluded in 1991. These had the result of making sampling, effectively free as of 1988, prohibitively expensive; the judge's decision in the most significant case began, "Thou shalt not steal."[21]

The accelerated culture war on hip-hop starts, arguably, with the obscenity charges filed against a clerk for selling a 2 Live Crew cassette to a minor in 1987; it blossoms with 2 Live Crew's 1989 album *As Nasty as They Wanna Be,* which generated a staggeringly extended and complex legal history—including a trailing suit for sampling practices. Taken together, these render uniquely apparent the unity of aesthetic, legal, and cultural attacks.[22]

Given the critical and legal pressure brought to bear on sampling in particular, it would be impossible to overvalue the fact that hip-hop's Golden Age is the golden age of sampling as well. As Hank Shocklee describes the development of composition strategies over the decade, "Eventually, you had synthesizers and samplers, which would take sounds that would then get arranged or looped, so rappers can still do their thing over it. The arrangement of sounds taken from recordings came around 1984 to 1989."[23]

The struggle for aesthetic recognition which pursued traditional versions of musicality, and the new regime of expensive licensing which preferred artists supported by major corporations, had in different ways the eventual effect of undermining rap's character of reproduction-as-production—a *material* character inseparable, as we have seen, from its social content. The bond between musical production and the social base of disenfranchised and untrained artists had defined rap's genesis, as well as the development of self-empowerment discourses, Black Power, Black Nationalism, and confrontation as a mode; the counterrevolution beginning in the late eighties had the effect of sundering this bond.

However, in understanding how these showdowns husbanded the shift from Black Power to gangsta rap, one notes that gangsta scarcely appeared an accommodation to the culture war, and was in fact the recipient of renewed vitriol in the form of decency crusades. As we'll see, the pivotal moments of the culture war in this period nonetheless had the effect of disciplining gangsta's emergence in a specific and curiously narrow direction en route to becoming hip-hop's house style (which it remains, in considerable and calcified degree, to this day).

BOYZ IN THE HOOD ARE ALWAYS HARD

If the emergence of gangsta retrospectively appears as instant and absolute, that is a sign of its dramatic character. Nonetheless, canonical gangsta document *Straight Outta Compton*'s relation to the internalization of struggle is both ambivalent and incomplete.[24] The musical and lyrical territory of gangsta wouldn't be consolidated until the 1992 album by N.W.A. member/producer Dr. Dre (Andre Young), *The Chronic,* effectively bringing to an end the period of emergence, which can now be dated precisely to the span 1988–1992.

The internalization of struggle as a lyrical and musical trope was not conjured overnight within hip-hop, that is to say, any more than it was newly discovered as a cultural issue. Indeed, it had been building as social concern and as rhetoric throughout the decade, under the increasingly common term "black-on-black violence." Before 1980, the phrase had no currency in the media; by 1985, from 24 percent (San Francisco) to 82 percent (Cleveland) of articles on local violence used the phrase "black-on-black violence" in the text.[25] As has been well documented by social scientists, the reductive term is thick with cultural conservatism.[26] It is not, in other words, a phrase native to the African-American community, but one imposed from without. Over the course of the decade, the language of black-on-black violence led to further reductions, collapsing alleged criminals and "Black youth" as a generalized category of suspicion and hysteria, as "this generic kid in violent or nonviolent states ritually transgressed in deed or thought."[27] The Black youth became a living figure for the possibility of violence: "Bodies this way were made texts. They displayed identities collapsed into revealing exclamations, looks, strolls, and movements."[28] The audience for these media narratives was invited to read Black bodies, but at a distance, and to feel informed about the nature of the urban core, offered up as a "terrain of pseudo knowledge and fantasy projection."[29] That terrain, in turn, became one laden with possibilities for both contamination and containment.

It is no great difficulty to see the ways in which gangsta rap, however much it was itself anathematized by later cultural crusaders, partook of this social fantasia. The mode of Black Power and Black Nationalism imagined a confrontation at the border of ghetto and suburb, and purposed to reach across that border, from the boulevard to the bourgeois. Gangsta mode, contrarily, offered up the spectacle of Black youth and a Black underclass ensnared (and even reveling) in a world of immanent violence that retreated from borders of geography, race, and class—and turned the violence on itself. Internalizing the rhetoric along with the conflict so that it all seemed both to arise from and transpire within the urban core, gangsta acceded precisely to the logic of containment.[30]

If this begins to describe the anxieties and imaginations that gangsta played to, and thus to account for the timing and force of its rise, it doesn't get at the nuances and fissures present from gangsta's earliest moments. *Straight Outta Compton* was itself preceded by the song "Boyz N The Hood," performed by one N.W.A. member and written by another, Eazy-E (Eric Wright) and Ice Cube (O'Shea Jackson), respectively. An extended criminal picaresque (akin to Slick Rick's contemporaneous "Children's Tale"), its overture celebrates the vision of the young Black superthug wreaking ghetto havoc as a matter of course:

> Woke up quick at about noon,
> Just thought that I had to be in Compton soon—
> I gotta get drunk before the day begins,
> Before my mother starts bitchin' about my friends.
> About to go and damn near went blind,
> Young niggaz at the pad throwin' up gang signs—
> Ran in the house and grabbed my clip
> With the Mac-10 on the side of my hip.
> Bailed outside and pointed my weapon
> Just as I thought, the fools kept steppin'. . . .
> Then I let the Alpine play
> Bumpin' new shit by N.W.A.
> It was "Gangsta Gangsta" at the top of the list,
> Then I played my own shit, it went somethin' like this . . .

The hyperbolic violence must be recognized as more than a bare accession to the conservative fantasy. The song's affect is one of uncontainable delight, paraded no more in the vocal than in the clangorous guitar samples and a profoundly deep bass easier to feel than hear. The song's exaggeration, its pleasurable excess, both registers and lampoons the contrivance of the young Black male as "America's nightmare."

Moreover, the emergent genre doesn't yet know enough to limit itself to black-on-black violence, and the song ends in an armed showdown with the judicial system. Historian and journalist Jeff Chang stages a superb reading of the lyric as containing within its comedy the tragic history of *Soledad Brother* George Jackson and his brother Jonathan, killed at seventeen in a courthouse shootout.[31] The account, and the song, gesture at the more general preservation—for a time—of the mode of inter-group confrontation within gangsta.

Straight Outta Compton's decisively titled "Gangsta Gangsta" is a résumé of the tropes that would come to define the gangsta genre: "Takin niggaz out with a flurry of buckshots"; "Homies all standin' around, just hangin' / some dope-dealin', some gang-bangin'"; and perhaps the most durable phrase, the t-shirt–ready axiom "Life ain't nothin' but bitches and money." This last supplied an inside-out objectification. Gangsta offered up the figure of the violent Black youth as a character to be consumed (from a safe distance); in turn, that character was increasing required to objectify the world around him. This defensive objectification would become gangsta's *other* structuring principle: cartoon materialism, aligning with black-on-black violence to dominate rap's lyrical content.

If this seems a *volte-face* from Black Nationalist rap's demand for economic self-sufficiency, such is not entirely the case. Hip-hop remains "a cultural form that attempts to negotiate the experience of marginalization, brutally truncated opportunity, and oppression within the cultural imperatives of African-American and Caribbean history, identity, and community."[32] The particular focus on *having things,* on possession and dispossession, remains constant. What flips is the stance toward these fixed desires: from the tribulations of living in a land where the property and power are always elsewhere, to the long folktale of getting these things.[33] The song remains the same, but for the shift from a confrontation with economic brutality to a phantasmatic identification with same: *Get Rich or Die Tryin',* per gangsta's unerring instinct for the truth of capitalism.[34]

The emergent nonetheless must shadowbox the fading dominant. The chorus of "Gangsta" locates the song in relation to rap's political mode, concluding with a conscious rebuttal of high-flown rhetoric: a sampled woman's voice concludes, "Hopin' you sophisticated motherfuckers hear what I have to say."[35]

The phrase is telling. Gangsta's anti-sophistication is an unassailable principle. Rhymed couplets are the order of the day—not so much simple as actively signifying simplicity, and thus a kind of authenticity. This reality effect is matched by musical loops substantially less complex than those of the Bomb Squad, less technique-heavy than Rakim's DJ/producer Eric B. This is not to say that *Compton*'s production (by Dr. Dre and DJ Yella) is unambitious—rather, it returns to the verities of hook, bassline, and beat, in transit from New York's uptown hustle to a slower funk more attuned to

Southern California's boulevard car culture. No hip-hop at the close of the eighties can escape the police siren: "Gangsta" begins with it. Against the Bomb Squad's multifaceted use of such sounds, here the siren is reduced to a single, literal meaning: crime.

But to let "Gangsta" tell the whole story of *Compton* is to elide its moments of external confrontation, not yet entirely sublated into the new worldview. Thus "Fuck tha Police": a six-minute document of fury. The outlaw thrills of "Gangsta" and *Compton*'s title song are largely missing; instead, the track proceeds from an agitated, agitating loop punctuated by a periodic shriek that quite evidently summons the Bomb Squad style. It begins where "Boyz" ends, in the courthouse—but here the drama unfolds in the funhouse mirror, as the white cops stand accused. Ice Cube is the first to testify:

Fuck tha police comin' straight from the underground
Young nigga got it bad cuz I'm brown
And not the other color so police think
They have the authority to kill a minority ...

Fuckin' with me cuz I'm a teenager
With a little bit of gold and a pager
Searchin' my car, lookin' for the product
Thinkin' every nigga is sellin' narcotics

The dynamic of racial confrontation is straightforward enough, with moments of greater nuance ("don't let it be a black and a white one, cuz they slam ya down to the street-top: / Black police showin' out for the white cop"). Inevitably, the lyric retreats from its brush with social realism into the myth of the Black superman (especially once Ice Cube yields the mic). Moreover, in the end the cops stand not as agents of an oppressive regime in a systemic confrontation—as one would expect in Black Power and Black Nationalist hip-hop—but merely as another set of thugs in the thug game, a kind of unjust interference to be dispatched: "Without a gun and a badge, what do ya got? / A sucka in a uniform waitin' to get shot." The hood is the night in which all cows are gangstas.

Nonetheless, this surviving element of racialized confrontation, as opposed to black-on-black violence, is a truth of the album. There is yet a third current running through the disc, even more historically remote. "Something 2 Dance 2" and "Express Yourself" were designed to move the dance floor, with considerable success (the latter is well remembered for Dre's charming grammar-rock rhyme, "Blame it on Ice Cube because he said it gets / funky when you got a subject and a predicate"). The songs "were like echoes of Eve's After Dark or an Uncle Jam's party, relics of an age of innocence that the rest of *Straight Outta Compton* was about to slam the door on forever."[36]

This makes the album a peculiarly elegant expression of Raymond Williams's structure. The three songs "Gangsta Gangsta," "Fuck tha Police," and "Express Yourself" respectively represent gangsta, Black Power, and old school party rap: in 1989, hip-hop's emergent, dominant, and residual styles. Their preservation within a single collection makes evident the volatility of the moment and the particulars of the situation, which might be termed the *uneven development of gangsta.*[37]

DOOWUTCHALIKE

In such volatile moments, with one dominant toppling and another not yet consolidated, the field flies open, or at least so it feels. The period is scarcely the only one of expansive and strange experimentation—by default, for example, the early days of Old School are ripe with inventions workable and not, songs like "Rappin' Duke" (by the eponymous artist) and the collective adventures of the "Roxanne" series. In any period, moreover, a great proportion of rap exists beyond that moment's organizing structures—the kind of music often referred to as "pop rap," a term less indicative of its success than its deracinated eagerness to please (though these may accompany each other, as in MC Hammer's 1990 *Please Hammer, Don't Hurt 'Em,* then the best-selling rap album ever).

Nonetheless, the possibilities that come into view in this window are remarkable for their variegation, openness, uneven brilliance. This alone should be enough to suggest that periodization is in order—that something is happening here which wants a careful accounting. These possibilities can scarcely be enumerated: wry sex thug Tone-Loc, British soul-hopper Monie Love, the inimitable Biz Markie having a heyday (and a legal disaster), and a thousand more.

Some of the inventions are of course openly determined by external forces, as we've seen regarding hip-hop's embrace of jazz sounds and instrumentation, for which these years were doubtless the peak, capped by the elegiac bop of "They Reminisce Over You (T.R.O.Y.)," by Pete Rock and CL Smooth, with its dusty alto sax sample signifying not so much authenticity as nostalgia and loss, the heart of the song. The great achievement of rap's jazz age was the 1991 album *The Low End Theory,* by A Tribe Called Quest, which featured noted upright bass player Ron Carter and became a rare site of agreement among hip-hop's aesthetes and hardheads.

Other apparitions of the era arrived intertwined with the dominant and emergent modes, not least the relative proliferation of substantial female emcees. On the East Coast, Queen Latifah (Dana Owens) aligned her feminism with racial politics and reference to Five Percenter teachings on 1989's *All Hail the Queen;* in Los Angeles, the 1991 debut of Yo-Yo (Yolanda Whitaker), *Make Way for the Motherlode,* seized on gangsta's raw language to build an eloquently frank realism that, at some distance from black superman hyperbole, stands out as an achievement of gangsta with a difference.

But if these two leading female emcees seem largely to recapitulate with variations the regional, stylistic, and programmatic transfer of the moment, that narrative surely can't account for the unique apparition of Neneh Cherry and her largely forgotten masterpiece, *Raw Like Sushi.* Cherry set off a tempest in a teapot when she performed lead single "Buffalo Stance" on *Top of the Pops* at the end of 1988, gyrating in a manner held to be unseemly for a woman seven months pregnant. The song itself, released in a dozen mixes, would hit number three on the *Billboard* Hot 100—as well as topping the charts for Club Play, Dance Music sales, reaching number sixteen on the Rap charts and thirty on R&B/Hip-Hop Songs.

This begins to suggest the song's protean quality; at the moment, there was nothing like it. This would be true of the album as well, released in May 1989 with a series of singles modulating fluently and fluidly through the current soul-based forms, albeit without trace of template or habit—and rarely arriving at a familiar rap song, with the exception of the implausibly titled "Outre Risque Locomotive." The disc seemed to float above the category of genre, not oblivious so much as omnivorous and cheerfully unaffiliated. Perhaps this is explained by the British production crew's distance from U.S. style wars, and Cherry's background as a world-citizen, child of artists and avant-garde musicians. Certainly the easy liberty is one aspect of the moment, and its sense that all bets were off, the old rules in rubble and the new ones not yet set in stone. The situation, the players, the scene—this conjuncture allowed, as if incidentally, the squaring of the circle in twelve inches of vinyl that was "Buffalo Stance."[38]

Since the middle of the decade, the dream of the rap/soul hybrid had been a thousand producers' alchemical dream, and equally elusive. Even the most popular attempts, for example "Friends" by Jody Watley (featuring Eric B. and Rakim), seemed conjunctions of solder and rivetwork, main force in search of a groove. "Buffalo Stance" draws the two genres jointlessly toward a unified form, a soul shuffle accelerated toward house tempo, hi-hat and scratch coming over the top. Wound throughout, Cherry's vocal swivels smoothly from spoken aside to playground sing-song with straight rap breaks, the title phrase alluding to both a street fashion style and the b-boy's hip-hop pose—*top that*. And then there are the occasional demands, the most assertive of which is "Bomb the Bass, rock this place!" The phrase serves as a genre marker, the hip-hop formula in which the producer is invoked: in this case, the Brixton DJ Tim Simenon, already doing business as "Bomb the Bass" on the London dance scene. This will not be his last appearance in the story of 1989, for he is one of the characters able to traverse genres and movements within the subterranean currents of the moment.

If there is a counterpoint to *Raw Like Sushi*, equally inventive and ambitious, similarly distant from the genre's central drama but prolix where Cherry is measured, frenetic against Cherry's sinuous ease, this eccentric landmark falls as well in the interzone. The Beastie Boys and producers the Dust Brothers confabulated in 1989 the unparalleled achievement of kitchen-sink surrealism, *Paul's Boutique*. Its hundred-plus samples were uncleared and employed not toward the Bomb Squad's combat sublime, but toward citation, quip, and overarching playfulness. The album is rap as a kind of pop heaven, where the artifacts of mass culture have gone not to die but to live again in the hip-hop context. It is, finally, a privileged culture-is-my-playground position, which allows for much of its delight. *Paul's Boutique* is at once the acme and exhaustion of the free-sampling age, an example of what can be done when there's no need to find an affiliation, and the anarchic endgame of anything goes. It is of no small note that within this passage of time the Beastie Boys themselves were en route from one ethos to another, and the course of the change is by now as predictable as it is suggestive: from the bratty antagonisms of 1986's *Licensed to Ill*, the trio would exit the era as Buddhist pacifists. Nineteen eighty-nine, it seems, is where confrontation goes to die.

For all that, the most playful, absurd song of the era came from the Bay Area in the form of Digital Underground's "The Humpty Dance." Released in late 1989 in advance of the curious and inspired album *Sex Packets,* the delirious sex rap–cum–dance craze samples Funkadelic, takes cheap shots at rap superstar MC Hammer, and features Humpty Hump: a priapic Groucho Marx for hip-hop, alter ego of group auteur Greg "Shock G" Jacobs. The video also introduces future rap martyr Tupac Shakur, who appears with retrospective strangeness as a backup dancer. Tupac, child of a Black Panther, populizer of the credo "THUG LIFE," provides a fascinatingly ambivalent figure for the transition from Black Nationalism to gangsta. But the unfathomable, unlocatable delights of "The Humpty Dance" are in their own way just as telling regarding the peculiar uncertainties of the moment and the strange flowers that bloom off to the side: songs that don't care and don't need to, temporary blossoms in the suddenly cracked concrete of hip-hop, as elsewhere the new emergent form figures out how to run the street.

TONIGHT WE GET EVEN

This volatility within N.W.A. resolved itself as swiftly and schematically as it arose. The party rap faded of its own accord, as residual styles do. The dominant, however, could not be excised so easily. In late 1989, Ice Cube left the group over royalty disputes; this departure was just the same a historical necessity, a scission that had to happen so that gangsta could become itself. Cube declared his allegiances plainly enough: his 1990 solo album *AmeriKKKa's Most Wanted,* produced in New York by the Bomb Squad, cited *Do the Right Thing;* the track "Once Upon a Time in the Projects" seemed a verdict about the period's hemorrhaging of social reality into the gangster's fairytale. Shortly thereafter he would become a Muslim, ambivalently involved with the Nation of Islam.[39] The surviving N.W.A. and its largely L.A.-based co-conspirators were thus left to engineer the gangsta emergence toward its realized form.

Yet there is another way to narrate the purification of gangsta than by structural subtraction; it is in this process that we can see the real effects of the culture war. Some of the best-known episodes would wait for the mid-nineties: the Reverend Calvin Butts endeavoring to steamroll a pile of compact discs and cassettes in Harlem in 1993, and C. Delores Tucker's decency crusade with the National Political Congress of Black Women in the same year (shortly to join forces with former Secretary of Education William Bennett).[40] Notable about these encounters is that they repeat the logic of black-on-black conflict, culturally internal but presented for broad consumption—which perhaps explains their popularity in cultural memory. They themselves are gangsta.

Far more determining are the clashes clustering around the actual period of emergence. In 1989, the FBI advised N.W.A.'s label regarding the song "Fuck tha Police"; the Fraternal Order of Police voted a boycott of the group (and of others advocating assaults on officers) and broke up a Detroit concert where they tried to perform the song. As gangsta moved from emergent to dominant style, larger social tensions were amplified first by the videotaped

Figure 4. Colored People Time with N.W.A.: "Straight Outta Compton." (Video dir. Rupert Wainwright, Priority Records)

police beating of Rodney King on March 3, 1991, and then by the riots and conflagrations following the officers' acquittal at the end of April 1992. As urban theorist Mike Davis emphasizes, the events shouldn't be simplified: "L.A. was a hybrid social revolt with three major dimensions. It was a revolutionary democratic protest characteristic of African-American history when demands for equal rights have been thwarted by the major institutions. It was also a major postmodern bread riot. . . . Thirdly, it was an interethnic conflict—particularly the systematic destroying and uprooting of Korean stores in the Black community."[41]

Jeff Chang argues that, for the purposes of media representations, it was a race riot "with Blacks centrally cast as Blacks and Korean-Americans in the role of the long-gone whites."[42] That the African-American community was geographically constrained from confrontation with whites is evident and suggestive. Against that containment, the riots' overflowing the boundaries of black-on-black violence was exactly the source of their intolerability. In the arena of hip-hop, this specific shadow-conflict had already come up for discipline at the end of 1991. In an unheard-of event, *Billboard* editor Timothy White called for a store boycott of Ice Cube's *Death Wish,* an album thick with misogyny and racialized violence, much of it directed toward fictive Korean-Americans.

In the same year, Ice-T (Tracey Marrow, "inventor of the crime rhyme")[43] started the hardcore band Body Count, whose eponymous debut included the song "Cop Killer" (which took up the repeated chant "Fuck the police" and ended "cop killer—but tonight we get even!"). Before being dropped from their record label, the band suffered a series of threats and censures, and eventually solicited the epic theater of Charlton Heston reading the lyrics of their song "KKK Bitch" in a Time Warner shareholder's meeting.

The coherence of these disciplinary actions is as evident as it is unremarked. In the case of each song and album, the intolerable transgression is *inevitably an episode of interracial violence.* If one accepts the tactical equivocation of whites and Korean-Americans within conservative and reactionary discourse, the dynamic is even plainer: black-on-white violence is what must be punished.[44] Images of equivalent violence within the Black community drew little commentary and no equivalent outrage.

Of course, the songs in question inevitably proposed this violence as retribution for a violence that historically ran the other direction. This can only have exacerbated the cultural reaction and punishment. Within the crucible of the moment, one can see this punitive reaction both as an expression of outrage and as a systematic effort to shape gangsta's emergence within this moment of malleability.

History, one might say, is the history of making politics turn away. We can see the culture war working not to stop gangsta, but to contain it—literally. Hemmed in on all sides *but one,* gangsta was in effect disciplined to turn its antisociality along the course of least resistance: to comply with and celebrate an account of Black urban culture which served the ideological ends of that culture's conservative critics, without being able to confront those very same antagonists. Black-on-black violence, the internalization of conflict, was not the only impulse present within gangsta's emergence, but the only one that would be given free reign.

JUST CHILL TILL THE NEXT EPISODE

Straight Outta Compton was dependent on the tensions and uncertainties of its moment, the particular structure in which the album was made, popularized, reviled. For emergent to become dominant, the spirit of gangsta had to be precipitated out. In 1991, Dr. Dre departed to start his own label; with 1992's *The Chronic,* Dre established himself as the sonic architect of a freestanding house of gangsta and, in concert with collaborating emcee Snoop Doggy Dog (Cordozar Calvin Broadus Jr., later simply Snoop Dog), the author of a worldview.

The structural black-on-black violence takes a tellingly specific form on the single "Fuck wit Dre Day (and Everybody's Celebratin')," a retaliatory volley at former bandmate Eazy-E, as well as New York rapper Tim Dog and Luther "Luke" Campbell of 2 Live Crew. The latter pair had insulted West Coast rap and Dre himself, respectively; Eazy-E, the song's main target, stands accused of dubious business dealings as head of N.W.A.'s label, Ruthless Records. Turf, masculinity, business—these will be the terms of gangsta's internecine rap battles, each song a "lyrical gangbang," as one *Chronic* title has it. Add to this the casual misogyny and homophobia that masculinity under siege seems to require, and poverty's fantasy of material wealth that will eventually be known as "bling," and the possibilities of gangsta stand before us. Chang hears it as "guiltless, gentrified gangsta—no Peace Treaties, rebuilding demands, or calls for reparation, just the party and the bullshit."[45] Such a verdict is accurate except insofar as Dre's "g-funk" turned out not to be a subcategory of gangsta but its apotheosis, what gangsta looked and sounded like once its held-over traces of social investment had been removed. The basics are summarized in a brief passage from *The Chronic*'s "Let Me Ride":

> I make a phone call my niggaz comin' like the Gotti boys
> Bodies bein' found on Greenleaf
> With their fuckin' heads cut off, motherfucker I'm Dre
> So listen to the play-by-play, day-by-day
> Rollin' in my '4 with 16 switches
> And got sounds for the bitches, clockin' all the riches
> Got the hollow points for the snitches

This is largely a clarification of the gangsta already found on *Straight Outta Compton,* with the ironic form of an inverted intensification. The lurid dramas of "Boyz N The Hood" or "Fuck tha Police" return as everyday life, nothing to get too worked up about—"just chill till the next episode," per the accurately casual "Nuthin' but a 'G' Thang." The gangsta picaresque is now distended infinitely across songs, groups, and years. In some regard this is what "genre" means.

This vision is not an independent source of the album's authority, which comes (just as with Public Enemy) from devising an expressive sound that seems at once cause and effect of this new world, a slowed-down resetting of seventies funk for which George Clinton and Parliament/Funkadelic are axiomatic: at least eight of their songs are sampled on *The Chronic*.[46] The effect is a sensual rumble led by a heavily modulated bass rolling beneath a higher-pitched synthesizer line, an improbable invention that felt as if a whole new affect had been discovered: easygoing menace. The sound is a kind of historical bookend to the Bomb Squad, both rupture and continuity: just as Dre's smoothed legato keyboard preserves Shocklee's keening siren as a distant memory, g-funk retains the sense of threat while breaking entirely from the sense of panic, of pressure at the bursting point. Here threat is not imminent but immanent, totally internalized. It is a way things are, and the players ride up and down Slauson Boulevard, vibrating the concrete.

Gangsta's worldview and the g-funk sound might also be seen as outcomes of the counterrevolution. The triumph of the crime rhyme is itself an inversion of the legal attack on hip-hop sampling starting in the late eighties. "Thou shalt not steal," began the judge's opinion; theft makes its mortal leap to the field of representation. The criminalization of rap returns as the rap of criminalization.

At the same time, the new sampling laws helped determine the shift from the Bomb Squad sound to *The Chronic*.

CHUCK D: Putting a hundred small fragments into a song meant that you had a hundred different people to answer to. Whereas someone like EPMD might have taken an entire loop and stuck with it, which meant that they only had to pay one artist.

STAY FREE!: So is that one reason why a lot of popular hip-hop songs today just use one hook, one primary sample, instead of a collage of different sounds?

CHUCK D: Exactly. There's only one person to answer to. Dr. Dre changed things when he did *The Chronic* and took something like Leon Haywood's "I Want'a Do Something Freaky to You" and revamped it in his own way but basically kept the rhythm and instrumental hook intact. It's easier to sample a groove than it is to create a whole new collage. That entire collage element is out the window.[47]

The force of the economic transaction in producing a song thus becomes audible in the song's aesthetic form and finally available as part of its content, in gangsta's fascination with material goods. "Economic self-sufficiency" is no longer thinkable by itself when a song can cost more to make than the median annual salary; this logic permeates all strata of thought. The age of the expensive loop is equally the age of hyper-fetishized commodity. *Bling* is the sound of a Bentley's headlights glinting off a $25,000 sample.

A NATION DIVIDED

Below the era's architects are lessers somehow more signal, more telling exactly for the way they ride the rhythms of cultural change, rather than trying to seize them in their hands. So it is with The Jaz (Jonathan Burks), sometimes Jaz-O and Big Jaz, a New York emcee of some local repute and no national presence who appeared in 1989, released the remarkable and ignored *To Your Soul* in 1990, a follow-up EP the next year, and was done.[48]

Song after song on *To Your Soul* is vital, serious, deeply musical, with playful lyrics that come at varying speeds, sometimes blunt and heavy on the beat, sometimes syncopated and sudden, looking for a way to slip past any defense. It's a kind of style-shifting that would become common later, virtuoso and then familiar and then just one of the ways hip-hop sounds. But in 1990 it was fresh, and it was the problem.

Or it was an evocation of the problem: The Jaz didn't know who he was. He didn't have a clear style or a sure point. He registers in this moment, as do so many pursuing popularity in their own moments, the forces at play— legion rappers led to sport kente cloth in 1988, prison chinos in 1992. The Jaz somehow contains all of this at once, or is buffeted by every possible wind. Now he's a Nation of Islam radical, with a spoken-word track called "Flag of the Mahdi"; now a thug with "a great white shark in my swimming pool." "I'm 6′3″, 210 and I keep funds comin' in," he announced, "this year the Max, next year the Benz." It's just at the edge of that exaggeration that would buy and sell the decade. His protégé with the strangely similar name, who appears first on this record, will achieve greater genre clarity: Jay-Z (Shawn Carter), who would work gangsta's logic until it mined and then mastered the organizational dominion of the corporate empyrean.[49] But in the summer of 1990, the future is still up for grabs. Nation time is ending. G-funk has yet to be perfected. You can still do the Humpty Dance. The

Wall is down. Exactly half the century so far has been before the Bomb, and half after. There are tanks in the Kuwaiti desert, and the Airborne is in Saudi Arabia. In a few months, Rodney King will be beaten with virulent brutality, on videotape, by L.A. cops. Everything, later, will seem to have been happening at once.

da inner sound, y'all

In 1989, the album of the year (per the broadest and most respected critics poll in the U.S., and *N.M.E.* in the U.K.) was hip-hop, but neither Black Power nor gangsta: De La Soul's *3 Feet High and Rising*.[1] The trio helped found the Native Tongues Posse, a collective with a long-standing relationship to the Zulu Nation that imagined a kind of third way ("three . . . is the magic number," one De La song insisted) both in social form and in social commitments: a "playful Afrocentricity" that was nonconfrontational and nonexclusive, neither cadre nor gang, neither radical politics nor black-on-black violence.[2]

Leery of both positions, the group cut a strange figure: "radically unlike any rap album you or anybody else has ever heard . . . playful, arch, often obscure, sometimes self-indulgent."[3] This may overstate the case. Nonetheless, the album's shifting musical palette and equally plastic thematic concerns register clearly a moment when the transfer between two dominant styles is incomplete. In formulating a relation to Black Nationalism and gangsta, *3 Feet High and Rising* is the reverse of The Jaz's *To Your Soul*, incoherent because it was free to choose neither rather than because it felt compelled to choose both.

This is not to say that the album is entirely sui generis or somehow outside of history; its comic eclecticism and manic play bear some relation to the anarchic charms of the Beastie Boys, while its penchant for jazz samples and rhythms partook of the then-current vogue. "Intellectual," "conscious," even "hippies" (a judgment they protested a bit too much)—in short, De La was hip-hop counterculture, generously enfranchised, bourgeois in both letter and spirit. This is the condition of their invention, which at its peak—the "Native Tongue Decision" mix of "Buddy"—rivaled any pop music of the era for untrammeled delight.

Beyond the songs' pleasures, the historical matter of *3 Feet High* is twofold. The first lies exactly in the way that the style constitutes a failed emergent. The tradition that Native Tongues pioneered survives through the time of this writing under various labels: "conscious rap," "backpacker," "undie-hop." It has, curiously, become a place where the remnants of black radicalism have taken shelter, largely with a less urgent manner than pre-1989 modes of hip-hop militancy. But it survives, just as the lattermost name has it, as an underground tendency. That an admittedly moderate, bohemian style could achieve both quite substantial commercial and critical success is peculiar enough; that this success was so ephemeral, finally an epiphenomenon of the shift from Black Power and Black Nationalism to gangsta, indicates clearly what kinds of positions could be popularly avowed only in this stretch.[4]

This locates De La Soul and crew in a sort of hip-hop genealogy of morals. But the Native Tongues worldview managed to engage, in this moment, elements that aligned it with other musical adventures altogether. In this it is utterly distinct from contemporaneous hip-hop, engrossed as it was in the intensities of its adolescence and the drama of the disenfranchised. The second historical matter is that of the Native Tongues' transatlantic kinship with the emergent form of the rave.

Part of this was musical: sonically adventurous, Native Tongues were more likely to experiment with the dance sounds then informing Britain's nascent acid house movement (including the Jungle Brothers' Todd Terry–produced 1988 crossover "I'll House You"). But the main juncture was ideological: the "positivity" and unity discourse that organized rave culture took the hip-hop guise of what De La Soul called "Da.I.S.Y. Age," the limping acronym standing for "da inner sound y'all." They issued a "Unity Mix" of the song "Say No Go" and a "House of Love" mix of "Me Myself and I"; they shared *Unity Mix 1991* with acid house leaders like The Shaman and The KLF.

Though careful not to appear too retrograde, the band was clear enough about the ethos: "We can have a psychedelic sound in some of our cuts, but we are *not* psychedelic rappers and we are not hippies. We just peaceful guys so we like to wear peace signs in our hair."[5] For all the disavowal, the social imaginary of De La Soul and Native Tongues was oddly of a piece with England's "Second Summer of Love." Countercultures, like happy families, are all alike.

CHAPTER 2

The Second Summer of Love

IT'S ALL STRUCTURE, but not the kind you can touch: structure like the economy or like belief, not like a factory. Postindustrial disco. At normal volume, the song is a bit otherworldly and curiously pacific, even flattened: a loping Afro-Latin rhythm built on a Roland 808 drum machine and 303 synthesizer, with a reverberating but somewhat distant woman's voice repeating careful syllables without sense, a spectral chant. It may be that she's been hypnotized. One male voice occasionally interjects "*la*-ter!"; a second, more frequent and varied, seems to be saying "voodoo ray."

That's the song: "Voodoo Ray," assembled in Manchester in late 1988 by A Guy Called Gerald, born Gerald Simpson. The woman is a regular co-conspirator, Nicola Collier; the two male voices are samples of British comedians Dudley Moore and Peter Cook, respectively.[1] At the proper volume, which is to say massive, it unfolds instantly, less pacific and otherworldly than infinite, a vast idiot sublime. Idiot is not an insult; it is beyond speech. If anyone is hypnotized, it's you. If anyone isn't hypnotized, they're missing something. "Voodoo Ray," which makes sense only on a dance floor, and mostly under the influence of Ecstasy, was the most popular independent single in the U.K. in 1989, peaking in July, at the beginning of the *second* Second Summer of Love.

The Second Summer of Love began in England in 1988 and by some accounts lasted through 1991, mapping almost exactly onto the present study.

Somewhat more strictly, the term designates the two summers of 1988 and 1989; the first when the rave scene was aborning, the second when it came into its own as the engine of youth culture in the U.K.

Rave is itself a periodizing term. It means something in 1989 that it hasn't meant before, and will be largely emptied of meaning shortly thereafter. As Simon Reynolds put matters in the indispensable study *Generation Ecstasy,* "In 1988 the word 'rave' was in common parlance, but mostly only as a verb, e.g., 'I'm going out raving tonight.' By 1989 'rave' was a fully fledged noun."[2] This linguistic conversion, in all its suddenness, corresponded to a shared experience of the subculture's early participants, of an "overnight Year Zero transformation of tastes and values."[3]

As we have already begun to see, the musical instances that this book tracks are invariably haunted by terminological shifts, debates, and uncertainties. Surely the taxonomy of popular culture is always written on the water; the foaming churn and roil around this period can't help but attract our attention as evidence of amplified transformation and instability.

Seen from the schematic distance of genre history, the rave era is a brief period of contraction, in which three underground streams of U.S. dance music briefly seem to reach a confluence in England under the name "acid house," before splitting into a dozen rivulets, and then splitting further. Closer inspection reveals, as it will, that absolute unity is always a mirage, a seeming. And yet such a sudden genre unification at the very moment of the Fall of the Wall—even if, *especially* if, it's just a seeming—would be occasion enough for this chapter, a way of thinking structurally about genre maps and political maps.

But the ethos of the rave can't help but interest us as well: a cultural politics formed as the genre was formed, around unity, both of these approaching coherence only for a brief moment. So: acid house and rave designate intertwined musical and social forms, which mutually constitute a subculture. This double-determined dynamic proposes the *emergence of unity:* a momentary unification that makes the apparition of rave so suggestive for thinking about 1989. "Year Zero," indeed.

LIFE IN A NORTHERN TOWN

By some accounts, Manchester is the rightful home of rave. So it's claimed in the 2002 Michael Winterbottom film *24 Hour Party People,* a morbidly antic faux-documentary of Manchester's musical history that takes its title from a song by native sons Happy Mondays. The story begins, inevitably, with the apostolic moment of the Sex Pistols' 1976 show at the Lesser Free Trade Hall and the tiny audience of disciples who hold the seeds of the city's musical flowering: The Buzzcocks, Joy Division/New Order, Morrissey of the Smiths, Simply Red, the producer Martin Hannett, and Tony Wilson—the last of these a television host and incipient music mogul whose character, despite his somewhat haphazard mien, serves to give some order to the film's stumbling narrative.

The real Wilson even had a theory that situated 1989 in an implicitly Oedipal cycle of rebellion and repression. "I was 13 in the school playground when the Beatles happened, I was 18 and went to university when the revolution in drugs happened, and I was 26 and a tv presenter with my own show when punk happened. And then I happened to still be alive when I was 38 when Acid House happened. Because it's a 13-year cycle . . . 1950—1963—1976—1989 . . . my big ambition is to be around for 2002 when the next thing happens."[4]

As an account, it's more nuanced than the local t-shirts that proclaimed "Woodstock '69, Manchester '89" (though, as we'll see, the invocation of the hippie past was crucial to rave's vision). Still, Wilson proposed his "thirteen-year cycle" theory in the nineties; there's little credit in being a prophet of what has already happened. Using a historically richer analytic in 1986, Wilson was a bit more able to see the future. "I saw Malcolm McLaren last week in Los Angeles, and his theory at the moment is that it will never happen again. He's saying that there are now so many avenues open to music that there's just no chance. I said to him, 'Just like fucking Lenin, right? There's a continuous dialectic going on until you've had your bit. As soon as you're in charge, that's the end; no more world revolutions.'"[5]

For all his seriocomic erudition, Wilson was most notable not as a wit but as founder of Factory Records and the Haçienda. The latter was a nightclub named from a passage in the estrangingly poetic utopian text "Formulary for a New Urbanism" by Ivan Chtcheglov—a novelty song of a manifesto for the Situationist International.[6] In July 1988, following on the mild success of their Nude parties, Haçienda started a night called Hot, with a swimming pool on the dance floor and sounds imported from the clubs of Ibiza (along with music from locals like Gerald and 808 State).

Such a commingling of utopia and hedonism would pervade the sensibilities of rave culture, along with the effects of Ecstasy and the corresponding need for unregulated spaces where this new world could be invented—an invention that extended beyond club hours. "That whole period just felt so special because no one had a clue what we were doing," recalled Mike

Pickering, one of Hot's DJs. "The authorities didn't have a clue. We used to come out of the Haçienda when it finished and go back to the Kitchen in Hulme, which was just two old council flats knocked together."[7]

In the end, the city's best-known contribution to rave would be the "baggy" sound developed by the live bands of "Madchester," named for "loose-fitting clothes, a loose-minded, take-it-as-it-comes optimism, a loose-limbed dance beat descended from James Brown's 'Funky Drummer.'"[8] Foremost among these were Happy Mondays and Stone Roses, distinct but for their birthplace. Predating the Second Summer of Love by a handful of years, the Mondays nonetheless found their likeness and logic there. They attempted literally to flesh out rave's promised pleasures: a sound system *both for and of* wasted lads, for whom the demented excess of the party was the only tolerable end, and better endless.[9] The Roses might be described as musical history's attempt to reaffix acid house to the guitar band; while their monumental self-titled 1989 album felt to many like a culmination of rave's ascent, it appears equally as the wellspring of a later phenomenon, Britpop.

Both acts are nonetheless attempts to grasp the moment and figures through which the subculture tried to do the same. The Stone Roses clung to "the perilously vague creed of 'positivity,'" while Happy Mondays endeavored to embody the shambling hedonism peculiar to the brief age. Both of these are aspects of rave's set of ideals. Nonetheless, it would be a mistake to seek the ideological moment in any given band, any given song, just as it would be a misrecognition to accept any singular origin city as cradle to the rave.

Manchester, once the foremost industrial city in the Western world, stands in complementary relation to London: one a massive, stolid national city representing domestic values; the other a world city, gleaming, vital, but with an international character viewed with suspicion in the provinces. This is caricature, of course, but it gets at the dynamic. London's cultural crossroads provided the global materials and laboratories to develop acid house as a style, but in 1988, with "rare groove" having its night in the clubs, going raving was one option among many. In Manchester, to invoke Thatcher's iron phrase, there was no alternative; the city's postindustrial ennui and cheaper spaces provided the conditions for the rave party to develop as a concrete phenomenon.

As it happened, acid house parties—raves—would realize and then consume themselves in a renegade felo-de-se that took place in neither city, in no city at all. But that is getting ahead of the story.

The three streams channeling into rave were Chicago house, Detroit techno, and New York garage. Their Atlantic crossing included a detour through the Mediterranean, through the open-air clubs of Ibiza. It was this "Balearic" style of house music that caught on in London, at Paul Oakenfold's club Future and then at the Ramplings' Shoom, at the end of 1987. But it was not just a musical style; it was a worldview, or wanted to be: "The Shoom ethos was love, peace and unity, universal tolerance, and we-are-all-the-same."[10] Reynolds's verdict gathers the nearly universalized codes of the scene. Superstar DJ Pete Tong recalled the early London club nights similarly, rattling off ethics and objects without distinction: "It was all one love, everyone together. Anyone can dance all of a sudden, freedom of expression. Dress down, not up. Converse trainers, smiley T-shirts—a sort of tribalism took over. Everyone was happy to be the same."[11]

The genre's formation was not entirely without a process. Hard upon importation, the Balearic sound ran up against "full-on acid house," with its cry of "acieed!" and its "Acid Teds," the young clubbing rabble derided by the cognoscenti. The Balearic style was identified with a kind of laid-back gentility and a jet-set cosmopolitanism, acieed with a more frenzied will-to-party, its devotees more local and lower-class. The globe and the street.

This offered a miniature of London's character as a world-city Cerberus: economic capital, cultural capital, global capital. It was the mutual pressure of Balearic and early acid house that drove the development of London's social scene and, shortly, an indigenous sound for acid house parties. While "acid house" swiftly won out as the genre's trade name, and the idea of an "acid house revolution" entrenched itself in the public imagination, still the musical double-formation of London's rave scene shouldn't be abandoned altogether. Within it is preserved the dialectical kernel, the center of rave's development.

In 1988, this development was swift, and accelerating. Club nights blossomed in size from the hundreds to the thousands. After Shoom's success, the London clubs opened like gates at the Epsom Downs starting bell: Spectrum, the Trip, R.I.P. This last, originally an underground club night and then a relatively aboveboard and frenetically popular venue, captured in its name another peculiarity of rave's doubled consciousness, not musical but explicitly cultural: an identification both with the supposedly *engagé* counterculture of the American sixties and with an isolationist hedonism.

Figure 5. The decentered DJ and the madding crowd: revolution in progress. (Photo Christian Kadluba)

At the time, it was commonly held that the club's name stood for "Rave In Peace"; in point of fact, it was an acronym for "Revolution In Progress." It remains hard to decipher whether these two slogans were congruent or contradictory, and if the latter, which carried the day. Journalist Sheryl Garratt's memoir, *Adventures in Wonderland,* frames the early London scene: "Many were using acid as well as Ecstasy. This, the longer hair, Ibiza's hippie past and the feelings of peace and love they felt they were sharing all invited parallels with the sixties, although without the radical politics."[12] In Reynolds's summary, "For all the self-conscious counterculture echoes . . . acid house was a curiously apolitical phenomenon."[13]

But apolitics is a politics—a fact that is always with us. Perhaps more importantly in the present case, many of the denizens of rave's growing scene *believed* it had a politics, and this matters. That "Rave in Peace" and "Revolution in Progress" could be understood as something other than contradictory is a useful first judgment on rave's social substance (and perhaps a judgment on the sixties counterculture's as well). A peaceful revolution, *revolution without conflict,* might be seen as the soul of rave's social desire.

Such a desire carries with it its own contradictions—contradictions that were managed with idealism and Ecstasy consumed in varying doses, without much clarity concerning which came first. It's worthwhile to attempt to catch this dual development in flight, for rarely has a subculture's self-identification been so thoroughly indexed to a single drug.[14] The reverse is true as well; one of the most comprehensive studies of the usage of what is more formally known as MDMA (and less formally as E, XTC, or X) was conducted through the British dance music monthly *Mixmag*.[15]

The Greek *ekstasis*—as is often mentioned—means "standing outside one-self." This state certainly aligns with Ecstasy's capacity for offering social intimacy, the escape from one's own restraints into the unity of the crowd. It gets as well at complementary and less-remarked-upon sensations, such as the occasional feeling of ecstatic alienation from one's ego, the paradoxical experience of euphoric melancholy that can typify especially the later portions of the E trip (as opposed to the obliterating elation of "coming up"). A strikingly beautiful orchestration of this feeling forms one of the era's earliest masterpieces: Electribe 101's "Talking with Myself," its title reverberating with this curious late-night affect. *Echo* is the name we have for literally talking to yourself. Echo, delay: these are ecstasy's digital analogs, a sound at once there and not, standing outside itself.

Electribe 101 spanned the period at hand and scarcely more, forming in 1988 and disbanding in 1992 with a second album unreleased. The group arranged itself in the disco tradition of studio whiz–meets–exotic diva, with the former role filled by four electronic composers from Birmingham and the latter by Hamburg-born Billie Ray Martin. Raised in London and Berlin, she would go on to considerable acclaim under her own name, though nothing would even approximate that first single, released in 1988 and carried into London on a Balearic breeze. The five-note vamp that opens the song is borrowed from Lalo Schifrin's *Mission: Impossible* theme, as is much of the music that unspools beneath Martin's echoey longing. Her voice is beside itself. "And if it's alright with you, I'll just talk with myself—I never was the one to leave you mad," she begins. "And when the light's shining down on you, you sure look tragic too." But the song's melancholy, its sense of something having been lost, is itself at a distance—held at bay by the beauty of Martin's voice, the heavy delay forming an invincible sheath. "The stars so bright and the light shine down and everything blows all around, it's a wonder world and a perfect time for loving tonight." The song finds the deep contours of the

Ecstasy trance's faraway-near, filling your head even as it sounds ten thousand miles away.

As acid house developed, it was increasingly designed to stimulate ecstatic ravers along a varieties of axes (and axons) that appealed to the sensual and/or emotional aspects of the Ecstasy experience. The preferred modulations and filters of the TB-303 sound produced the sonic core, and the development of less linear song structures led the formal developments. Stravinsky defines music as an alternating succession of exaltation and repose; acid house, particularly in its more ambient guises, moved to synthesize these into a unity and even a textured uniformity: an ambience, an atmosphere, to which the experience of Ecstasy was better suited, a *both/and* of exaltation and repose at once.

The titles and lyrics making more and less explicit reference to the drug and its effects are innumerable; following the countercultural tradition, barely coded references became bonds in a knowing collectivity. The music was thus compelled to understand and fashion itself as a drug, as an aid to a shared experience rather than as an end in itself; this dynamic of communion aligned with a predictably escalating spiritualist aspect to the rave.

For a while this triangulation of consciousness around music, drugs, and spiritualism still allowed for the coexistence of high seriousness and high comedy—a balance indicative of rave's high era, when meanings were still fluid. The blossoming scene, the music's mutating inventiveness, the rush of E—all of these supplied a sense of abundance, of excess in the experience that hadn't yet been ordered, managed, made doctrinal. In 1989, the Orb could at once proffer and mock the rave's ecstatic technospiritualism in the title of their charting single, "A Huge Ever Growing Pulsating Brain That Rules from the Centre of the Ultraworld (Loving You)," found on a disc labeled "Ambient house for the E generation."[16]

Even such gentle ironies as this could be fleeting. Rave's ubiquitous smiley face, resuscitated from the seventies and often printed on tabs of E, might have been a tacit admission of the good time's contentlessness. For many, it became the content itself, symbol for the distinctly unironic communal virtue of being "loved up."[17]

The attempt to recognize what felt new in this particular intersection led to what was, in effect, "a novel therapeutic class" for *3,4-methylenedioxymethamphetamine* and its brethren—one that indexed Ecstasy's chemical effects to the social form of the rave crowd. This new class was dubbed the "empathogen-entactogen," characterized by an empathetic capacity for increased social connection and a greater access to one's own emotions: "The effect of these drugs," one researcher observes, "was to enable the therapist—or patient—to reach inside and deal with painful emotional issues that are not ordinarily accessible."[18] Such rhetorics of openness, of the removal of barriers and boundaries, are ubiquitous in the literature, scientific and otherwise: "If punk's negativism was really poisoned romantic utopianism, that blocked idealism flowed free in the 1990s thanks to Ecstasy," writes Reynolds.[19] "The basic effect is to lower the defenses," notes a scholarly overview, making sure to tack on a caveat: "while this may be useful in psychotherapy and enable the person using it to let go and feel good, it can also be very destructive."[20]

It presents little difficulty to recognize the alliance of ideology and pharmacology in such reports, through which the subjective, contingent qualities of the acid house revolution are provided an objective, clinical rationale that is itself seemingly universal and nonhistorical—as if rave culture could have appeared at any moment, given the fortunate collision of a certain music and a certain scientific excitation of serotonin and dopamine levels. This chemical universalism peeks forth from the code of community values that appeared at the beginning of the nineties, LPE: *Love Peace Ecstasy*. This credo would shortly morph into the more easily murmurable acronym PLUR: *Peace Love Unity Respect*. That "Unity" and "Respect" should make a suitable replacement for "Ecstasy" is telling enough.

Reynolds himself, with his considerable theoretical sophistication, dwells little on rave's place in the historical fabric. He does not ignore such matters entirely, and his select asides are well taken: "It's no coincidence that Ecstasy escalated into a pop cultural phenomenon at the end of the go-for-it, go-it-alone eighties (the real Me Decade). For Ecstasy is a remedy for the alienation caused by an atomized society." For Reynolds, notably, the acid house revolution is often attached to history by molecular chains: "Ecstasy had catalyzed an invincible feeling of change-is-gonna-come positivity, seemingly substantiated by events across the world like the downfall of Communism."[21]

Even more suggestive is scene chronicler Richard Smith's 1989 description of loved-up nights at Trade, a gay club in London, as being a "communism of the emotions."[22] However eloquent such a comment might be, it's hard to miss its symptomatic quality—not despite, but because of the absence of any reference to the world events unfolding in parallel. These blind spots insist on rave's imagination of itself as outside of history, as existing in "the unconfined unreckoned year" of the Second Summer of Love, the very datelessness of which is now seen as entirely necessary to such a self-construction.[23]

It should be understood that one function of "unity" as a politics is exactly to render continuous this timeless communism of the emotions with the relentless capitalism of reason which drove rave culture forward along its developmental arc. Like any developing economy, the rave was compelled to seek out less confining and less regulated frontiers. In practice, this meant decamping from the city for the expansive fields and warehouses arranged around the new road ringing the outskirts of the city. Farewell, then, to London scenemaking. And farewell to residual elements of exclusivity associated with the Balearic style, nights of closed-door clubs, semiofficial dress codes, and admission policies. Unity, as distinct from solidarity, can only progress by internalizing adherents. Unity must keep astounding itself with greater and greater numbers; in rave's 1989, gigantism was the order of the day.

NEOLIBERAL ORBITAL

The ring road in question, the M25 Orbital, is as much an organizing principle as a place, as much a symbolic workhorse as an organizing principle. Round like a DJ's turntable—that won't quite do. Round like a 12″ vinyl remix with its spindle hole in the middle, literally decentered—that's better, hold that thought. A place for loved-up kids to rave in peace, the ring road's loop is a literal revolution in progress (always already, as they say). It's a spatial analog for the rave's psychedelic/amphetamine fantasy of timelessness, the limitless trance-dancing, and the relentless rhetoric of the "eternal." Its infinite circularity makes, correspondingly, a fine figure for the endless looping of the acid house song, the formal logic of iteration/recursion/cycle, as opposed to the common pop song's separate parts, its linear progression toward tonal resolve and formal closure. The night, the music, and E: ambient like an ambit.

The M25 Orbital's name haunts the history of acid house, by reason or by chance. In addition to the aforementioned Orb, there was William Orbit, more ambient still, who would eventually come to international fame as a producer of Madonna's foray into British electronic sounds, *Ray of Light*. More immediately, the ring road donated its name to one of the era's most popular and critically admired acts, the two brothers known as Orbital. Their first single, 1989's homemade "Chime," would land them on *Top of the Pops* in one of the rave's mainstream breakthroughs and serve as a blueprint for more heavily produced electronic anthems. It's in some regard the offspring from Kraftwerk's marriage of machine-disco and the autobahn, but the circular logic of the Orbital road is even more determining of the songform. Voiceless and progressing through careful textural variations with a

Figure 6. M25: the Orbital by night. (Photo © Jason Hawkes/Corbis)

calm cyclical drive that eventually accrues an epic feel through sheer force of duration and insistence, "Chime" is the ring road as a synth loop.

As a place where the Acid Teds reinvented the scene-hopping mobility of the Balearic crowd without abandoning the Home Counties, the M25 offered a conceptual bridge: the globe and the street all at once. A sort of vernacular cosmopolitanism. The ring road figured even better the decentered dream of the rave, where the crowd—ten, twenty, thirty thousand—was the star, the artists/DJs not focal points but mere enablers. Here we have arrived at something like the material code for rave ideology: inclusivity without distinction, mobility without direction, a party without end in which the adamantine antinomies of global and local, stage and floor, performer and audience, exaltation and repose, chorus and verse, figure and ground are battered down like so many Chinese walls. But it is the year of the Berlin departitioning that is at stake: as a symbolic figuration of unity and infinite motion, the architecture of the ring road stands as the very opposite of a wall.[24]

Then again, as an image of circulation itself, the Orbital stands just as well for late capitalism's endless murmur of motion as it circles the world without restriction. The structural echoes of Thatcher's neoliberal revolution within the acid house revolution were not lost on some of rave's savants. "Anarcho-capitalist" promoter Tony Colston-Hayter of Sunrise, cynical pioneer of the

Orbital rave, was prepared to leverage Tory values for the right to party all night, behind the logic that the economy never closes: "Surely this ridiculous three AM curfew on dancing is an anachronism in today's enterprise culture."[25] One is hard-pressed to decide whether to fill in the eccentric circle of the M25 on the Great Britain road atlas with a peace sign, a smiley face, or a day-glo dollar sign. Not for the first time, the alternatives made common cause.

In practice, the M25 offered not just accessibility to London at a spacious remove from the city's super-densities; it also provided a mechanism for keeping rave locations secret, unannounced until the last second, and movable if need be. This in turn allowed the parties, for a while at least, to stay ahead of the police, who finally weren't quite neoliberal enough to smile on an escalating tax-free trade with a parallel market in class A drugs, and with a high nuisance rating to boot. (The abject days of rave would see the Criminal Justice and Public Order Act of 1994, with a special section on raves in which outlawed music is defined as "sounds wholly or predominantly characterised by the emission of a succession of repetitive beats.")[26]

Such a hide-and-seek utopia couldn't last; gigantism can't help but pursue its own limits. The heroic era of the Orbital rave rose mercurially and scattered. Over the course of 1989, promoters such as World Dance, Genesis, Helter Skelter, and Energy succeeded in setting acid house nights free of the urban core's constrictions, staging ever more elaborate Orbital parties in borrowed and rented fields, the odd warehouse, or some other similarly vacant megastructure. It was as if the organizations were staggering around London's outlands in the dark, impelled by material circumstances to discover through blind sense of touch the underused and abandoned spaces of England's pastoral and industrial past and make them live again.

Biology, which had held their first party in February at a film studio in Battersea with three thousand in attendance, drew ten thousand to some Watford farmland a few months later. First-generation acid house sorts— Shoom, the rave zine *Boys Own*—attempted their own Orbital parties, but were unable to keep pace. Events were moving swiftly. On June 24, 1989, Colston-Hayter's Sunrise attracted eleven thousand ravers for Midsummer Night's Dream, held at an airstrip in Berkshire. At the end of September at a Helter Skelter rave near Oxford, the KLF would throw their night's pay into the crowd: Scottish pounds on which they'd written "CHILDREN WE LOVE YOU." The same night, a Phantasy rave outside Reigate drew an estimated twenty thousand; a police raid ended with the constables in full retreat before the hired security team Strikeforce.[27] Now things were really falling apart. In October, Biology made plans for a megarave in Guildford, to feature Public Enemy in addition to the usual suspects. Their ad on pirate radio ran thus:

> This is a Party Political Dance Broadcast on behalf of the Biology Party. Here are the following requirements for this Saturday's DJ Convention and gathering of young minds.... Firstly, you must have a Great Britain road atlas. Yes, that's a Great Britain road atlas. Secondly, a reliable motor with a full tank of gas. Lastly, you must have a ticket and you must be a member. So we now end this Party Political Dance Broadcast on behalf of the Biology Party. Don't waste your vote: stand up and be counted ... because ... BIOLOGY IS ON![28]

Tired pun on *Party* notwithstanding, it's hard to discern the level of intentional comedy in the call. The relatively serious politics of invitees Public Enemy signify one way; the inescapably ironic hijacking of rebel broadcasts and guerilla politics signifies another.[29] Even within that irony, the charge of having one over on the police is itself a political pleasure. But Biology's party was not to be. The location was moved repeatedly, trying to stay ahead of the law; the police eventually shut it down, turning away an estimated thirty thousand. This disaster signaled the end of the second Second Summer of Love, and of the underground Orbital rave—even as rave anthem "Ride on Time" celebrated six weeks as the most popular song in the nation.

ACID ON THE RADIO

"Ride on Time" wasn't the first number one acid hit; in fact, it was a kind of return to one of acid house's origin myths. S'Express's "Theme from S'Express" was acid house's debut at the top of the Top of the Pops in spring of 1988, having vaulted over more common fare like the crooned ballad "Mary's Prayer" by Scottish trio Danny Wilson.[30] "Theme from S'Express" begins with a Eurodisco synthesizer line of the sort pioneered in the seventies by Giorgio Moroder and Jean-Marc Cerrone; member Chilo Harlo intones "Enjoy this trip ... enjoy this trip ... and it is a trip," like the world's squarest tour guide, and the song is off and racing over a sampled Rose Royce bass line and house's standard four-on-the-floor drums. The vocal hook is an original, sung by American hip-hop diva Michel'le.

Retrospectively, various formal and thematic elements of acid house are already in place, including the decisive "playful reworking of that old travel motif" from Kraftwerk, which would be bent into a curve around the M25.[31] Hook-heavy and collage-happy (including a sample from performance artist Karen Finley), "Theme from S'Express" fit the tradition of announcing a subgenre's emergence into the arena of pop with what first appears as a novelty song. When the Timelords' "Doctorin' the Tardis" reached number one near the end of June, with its simpleminded collapse of the *Doctor Who* theme and Gary Glitter's crass anthem "Rock and Roll (Part Two)," its species resemblance to S'Express seemed only to confirm the novelty status of both. In addition to the publication shortly thereafter of a how-to manual based on the song, the Timelords' absurdist turn on *Top of the Pops'* year-end show scarcely challenged this verdict.[32] By comparison, S'Express (the only other electronic dance act to appear on the show) was rather serious: the "enjoy this trip" intro was censored by the producer, and Michel'le ended the song sitting on the floor in protest. "All of this combined is the best advertisement for Acid House and drug taking you could ever hope for," wrote group auteur Mark Moore in the *Guardian*. "Overnight the nation of Great Britain changes."[33]

"Overnight" overstates matters a bit. At the end of 1988, for all the unity of a given rave, a given club night, acid house had yet to achieve the atomized unification of disparate audiences for which the pop charts stand. It remained a nebulous outline beyond the pale of the mainstream, a peripheral rather than core element in the music industry and the public imagination. An attentive observer might have read the tea leaves, especially if she'd heard "Talking with Myself." The quotes from television theme songs alone might have given the game away, the jumble of sampled snippets and the closely cropped house diva howls. Industry market monitor *Billboard* was not so canny; a lengthy supplement in late July titled "Dance Music and New Music" noticed nothing afoot, mentioning "Euro house" only once and in passing.[34] As the Timelords exited the charts, the moment of novelty seemed to have passed. In October, England's leading radio outlet, Capital, announced Capital Gold, a twenty-four-hour oldies station attuned to the nation's nostalgia trend.[35] By the middle of autumn, Enya's "Orinoco Flow," Kylie Minogue's "Je Ne Sais Pourquoi," and Whitney Houston's "One Moment in Time" held the top three slots. In the open of the airwaves, the first Second Summer of Love had left things largely unchanged.

The few acid tracks that grazed the charts were half-measures, mainstream conciliations—until December, when Humanoid charted with something altogether different.[36] "Stakker Humanoid," a spooky, minimal sprint with no hook beyond a momentary splice from the video game *Berzerk*, gave little ground to pop conventions or the spirit of one-off amusement. Gone were the full vocal lines of Electribe, gone the kitschy bricolage of S'Express, the Timelords, or for that matter Bomb the Bass and M/A/R/R/S. But moments from each of these found a unity in "Stakker Humanoid," not a magnificent song but formally near perfect: a darkly reflective surface which held beneath it a sinuous energy that would flash forth momentarily—*throw your hands in the air*—returning straightaway to the depths, leaving the surface mutated.[37] This was the new, without the novelty.

Nonetheless, contra Mark Moore, 1989 began with little more than signs and portents. In retrospect, it's apparent that the nation was opening to dance music as a broader phenomenon—a sort of enabling condition for acid house's growth beyond subcultural boundaries. Soul II Soul's first hit, "Keep on Movin'," peaked at number five; "Back to Life (However Do You Want Me)" began the summer at number one. At the opposite end of the chart, "Voodoo Ray" snuck in at number forty. The clearest harbinger of acid house's breakthrough, however, wasn't a dance track at all. The week after "Voodoo Ray"'s debut, the aforementioned northern folk combo Danny Wilson charted with "The Second Summer of Love." After invoking the Dream Academy's winter's tale, "Life in a Northern Town," the song turns sunny: "Ah the first Summer of Love was here when I was much too young; the first Summer of Love was clearly just a summer long." The song is punctuated by the cheery chorus, culminating in "There was love love all over the country, love all over the world."[38] Its lone minor-chord passage follows, marking to market as pop bands must: "Acid on the radio, acid on the brain; acid in the calico, acid in the rain."

The song's half-repressed anxiety of industrial competition wasn't misplaced: the Second Summer of Love had finally arrived on the radio. As "Voodoo Ray" reached number twelve without major label support, Norman Cook (later known as Fatboy Slim) demonstrated his early grasp of lowest-common-denominator acid with "Won't Talk about It" / "Blame It on the Bassline." By the end of August, pop's upper reaches were as consolidated as industry allows, under the smiley-face flag. Lil Louis's panting "French Kiss" was at number four; Betty Boo and the Beatmasters' manic cartoon house, "Hey DJ / I Can't Dance (to That Music You're Playing)," was eleven; deep house diva Adeva stood at eighteen with "Warning!"; Detroit pioneers Inner City returned to the charts once again with "Do You Love What You Feel." And "Ride on Time," in only its third week, had climbed precipitously to number three. Studiously recreating the Rose Royce bass line of "Theme from S'Express" under an Italo-house piano sprint, Black Box built their diva hook from a Loleatta Holloway vocal sample—a shriek beyond ecstasy or agony, designed to blow through your head like a bullet train. This was unity as sheer domination, irrefutability with a disco beat. It occupied the top spot just as Technotronic's "Pump Up the Jam" entered; by October they would be one and two, and they would hold the high ground for another fortnight before starting to fade.

But the spell could not be broken. 808 State charted with "Pacific State," cowritten by already departed member A Guy Called Gerald—a slightly jazzy return to the more minimalist manners of "Stakker Humanoid" from a year earlier, as was Orbital's majestic "Chime," recorded in December ("winter acid," one might say). At the same time, Manchester's rave bands arrived in the public consciousness. Stone Roses peaked at eight with "Fool's Gold," while Happy Mondays' *Madchester Rave On E.P.* quite suddenly landed at number one. Christmas 1989, and rave had finally unified the pop charts.

3 A.M. ETERNAL

Having converted its impulse from unity of the shared event to unification of the abstracted market, rave could go in various directions, and it did. Which is to say that the story ends there. If rave is defined first by the process of unification, which is then displaced by the ideology of unity, this is realized by the end of 1989; time stands still in the hourglass of acid house, contracted at the neck. This moment arrives just as central Europe undergoes its initial wave of disunification from the Eastern Bloc; from mid-1990, acid house undergoes its own dissolutions and disarticulations. As Reynolds says, "What had once been a unified subculture based on a mix of musics began to fragment along class, race, and regional lines," with a stratification both of social scenes and musical subgenres, a proliferation which begins with the old schools of house, garage, and techno and then—after the acid house moment—moves into jungle, gabba, trance, happy hardcore, bleep-and-bass, breakbeat house, Belgian hardcore, speed garage, big beat, ambient techno, and atmospheric electronica.[39] For trainspotting taxonomists, this is only a beginning. Such thoroughgoing balkanization of genre—this, too, is of the moment.

The social form of the rave persists after 1989 as well, in similarly fragmentary terms. On the one hand, the corporatized rave endures as a choice among many, slotted into the leisure industry between (and even overlapping with) cruise ships and wilderness adventures. On the other, the renegade "teknivals," arranged by collectives such as Spiral Tribe, Bedlam, and DiY Sound System, remained outside the law. That these later figures were openly politicized, in contradistinction to rave's first generation, affirms the point: social negation is revealed as exactly what was absent from the spirit of the Second Summer of Love. Perversely, both these second-generation rave traditions find their afterlife in Nevada's Black Rock Desert, where today the annual Burning Man festival serves as a busman's holiday from the free market's intransigently capitalist anarchy.

Between emergence and residuum, a few striking moments stand out. Bill Drummond and Jimmy Cauty are in conjunction the red thread running through the Second Summer of Love, drawing together moment after moment with the glee of the conspiratorial—that secret unity known only to initiates and the paranoid. The two artists join forces in 1987 as the Justified Ancients of Mu Mu (the JAMS) and immediately encounter legal troubles for pairing sampled pop hits as new singles. In 1988, Cauty cofounds ambient house pioneers the Orb; later that year the duo is doing business as the Timelords, with acid novelty hit and acidulous how-to manual. By the summer of 1989, as the KLF, they're chucking Scottish pounds into the audience outside Oxford (an impulse that will return in 1994 for a supposedly career-capping performance, in which they incinerate a million pounds sterling of their own money—a charmingly boring spectacle conducted in semiprivate but captured on film).[40]

Amid all the madcappery, it's easily forgotten that this final configuration of Cauty and Drummond ended its musical run with a string of singles that tower over the genre (perhaps matched only by the more ascetic and intricate Orbital). Temporality is ever the pair's obsession—does not the name the Timelords, and the anachronistic samples they set loose, testify early on to a fascination with bending time to their will? This aligns exactly with what A Guy Called Gerald identified as the formal basis of rave's relation to the clock: "With a sample you've taken time. It still has the same energy but you can reverse it or prolong it. You can get totally wrapped up in it. You feel like you have turned time around."[41]

For the KLF, this logic permeates every level from production to profession, as in the duo's habit of releasing a given song in multiple iterations, compulsively, over the course of years—as if to confuse the teleology of the business, of the career. *Countertemporalities:* perhaps that gets at the matter. "What Time Is Love?," first distributed in 1988, reaches the top five in the fall of 1990 with the mix subtitled "Live at Trancentral," and again in 1991 as "America: What Time Is Love?" Their biggest hit, "3 A.M. Eternal," first appearing in 1989, tops the charts in 1991 with the "Live at the S.S.L." mix. When "Last Train to Trancentral (Live from the Lost Continent)" reaches number two later that year, the KLF becomes 1991's best-selling singles act in the world.

These three songs, in their achieved forms, make up the "Stadium House Trilogy." They take their name from their spectacular scale: reverberating and pseudo-live, mixing in oceanic washes of phantasmagoric crowd noise even as the tracks are studio-made and shipped to radio, recognizing the shift of the rave's center of mass from the club to the orbital party to the airwaves, the general space of commercial culture. The songs cannot resist simultaneously literalizing and lampooning the grandiosity of rave's utopian idealism and material success, the blind gigantism that is unity's endgame. They make a joke of contradiction.

The minimal lyrics—the titles, the chanted hooks—propose a rhetoric to revitalize acid house's discourse of nonlinearity. But even this monumental attempt to possess timelessness is a twilight form. The songs are in every regard an example of what pop music's "late style" must be: monstrous, ambivalent, towering above the genre exactly because it is too late to be *of* it. The very fact that the songs must announce in language what "Chime" or "Voodoo Ray" reached after in their shapes bespeaks belatedness. Still the songs are unrelenting in their dream against the tyranny of temporality. Every passage testifies to it, every title or phrase is a fragment of its unity. The exemplary "3 A.M. Eternal" names the desire unerringly, finally not just the KLF's but that of the rave, the acid house revolution: the desire for a time that is not in time, a *unity outside history.*

I Was Up Above It

For all acid house's roots in U.S. dance music, the specificity of the U.K.—its racial and interurban dynamics, its place in the circuit of European cosmopolitanism, the stone-gray particularities of the postindustrial landscape, of Thatcherian economics—must have much to say about how the rave became an adequate, even sublime response to the moment. An imitative rave culture gained little purchase in the native soil of house, techno, and garage.

The points of intersection, of oblique relation, will have their own say. Perhaps most suggestive among them was the later electronic apparition of "industrial," a metal machine music splayed across club beats. Largely American, the phenomenon was nonetheless international. British luminaries Nitzer Ebb were deeply imbricated in the genesis of acid house; the single from that band's 1989 album *Belief,* "Control, I'm Here," was a club hit. The album shared a British producer (Flood, né Mark Ellis) with the act that would turn out to be the genre's enduring exemplar: Nine Inch Nails, contrived by Cleveland native Trent Reznor, whose debut, *Pretty Hate Machine,* is one of the striking documents of 1989.[1] Much of the recording was done in London that year, acid house's Year Zero (a phrase that Reznor would use as a title almost two decades later for a dystopic concept album), as the atmosphere filled with Ecstasy.

Reznor's mode is closer to agony. The title alone excludes *Pretty Hate Machine* from the ethos of acid house. The songs are frequently more stripped and serrated than straight-up acid, much less the Balearic and older house styles; they also preserve traces of rock instrumentation and verse-chorus structure (a tradition never fully purged from acid house either). For all these differences, however, NIN shares a wealth of genetic code with acid house, especially the variation earlier called "winter acid." The sonic surfaces are gunmetal black, digitized until the individual electrons gleam darkly. Several tracks might be anxious replicant siblings of "Stakker Humanoid"—most obviously closing track "Ringfinger," with its cyclically mutating synthesizer line and condensed squelch. The last few seconds dissolve into a pulsing whirr of static; tuning in there, one might believe it was the latest bid for hardcore acid utopia.

The lyrics, however, come from a world alien to ecstatic clubbing: "Head like a hole! Black as your soul!" runs the chorus of the opening song; "I'd rather die than give you control!" Such cartoon negativity is rave's positivity in a camera obscura. Reznor seems to recognize this explicitly, reaching out to pierce the chiton of rave's ideology and reveal the exclusions implicit in its dream of unity: "god money let's go dancing on the backs of the poor."

But it is not finally enough to discover in *Pretty Hate Machine* some acid tracks and an inverted ethos. The inversion aligns with a particular turn common to a different emergent genre of 1989. The motion is thematized schematically in "Down in It." "Kinda like a cloud I was up way up in the sky and I was feeling some feelings you wouldn't believe," it begins, conjuring rave's euphoric, dematerialized space beyond the world. But something is wrong in this paradise, a paradise that is swiftly read as escapism: "Sometimes I don't believe in myself and I decided I was never coming down." We know that there will be no blissful drifting away. This is clear both from the stain of anxiety and from Reznor's delivery, all tuneless nervy crystal-meth chatter until it yields to his aggrieved, throttled scream (itself cousin to nothing in acid house, but relative to much of grunge's howlings). "I was up above it—now I'm down in it." Here, then, is ecstatic unity stood on its head: the song isn't about coming up but coming down, and "in it" doesn't mean joining the loved-up crowd. But neither is it a return to temporality, to history's real. Rather, it is down into the shit of the mind, the abject depths of the self. "I used to have something inside; now just this hole that's open wide." The hole is the head, as we've discovered. Into the hole we go, retreating from the social to the psychologized interior: the inward turn that will define grunge.

CHAPTER 3

Negative Creep

"LEARN NOT TO PLAY YOUR INSTRUMENT," Kurt Cobain wrote in his notebook in 1990, a slogan handed down from indie rock dogmatist Calvin Johnson.[1] That Cobain should cleave to this dictum has a certain aesthetic irony, given that he turned out to be an idiosyncratically remarkable guitarist. A further irony is that highly accomplished technical proficiency lay at the core of the metal genre that provided one of Nirvana's foundations; by all accounts, Black Sabbath and Led Zeppelin were formative influences, along with the more errant black metal of Celtic Frost. Nirvana's epochal *Nevermind* would be mixed by Andy Wallace, who had helped produce the estimable speed metal act Slayer.

There is nonetheless some element of actuality in Cobain's transcribed phrase; when *Nevermind* occupied the number one position less than three months after Guns N' Roses' epic *Use Your Illusion II,* it effectively put paid to rock's dominant tradition of guitar heroics. The virtuosic solo vanished from the radio as if at a single stroke. This describes in part the force of grunge's influence and innovation as a genre: it reconfigured not just the semantics of the rock song (the lyrical content or the emotional pitch, for example) but the syntactic structure.[2]

By the mid-eighties, metal had itself moved from parking lot subculture to mass market leader in the form of glam metal; luminaries included Bon Jovi, Motley Crüe, Poison, Warrant, and Skid Row (also an early name for

Figure 7. The creep stands alone: Kurt Cobain on the inside looking in. (Photo Marty Temme/WireImage/Getty Images)

the band that became Nirvana, as it happens). Sometimes known as "hair metal" or "nerf metal," the form was implausibly if variably slight, given its mythically heavy ancestry in psychedelic blues and antisociality, of which devil worship merely provided the semiofficial horn salute. Starting around 1986, already an industrial force, it went from strength to strength. In 1988, Def Leppard's *Hysteria* held the number one spot for much of the fall, yielding directly to Guns N' Roses' *Appetite for Destruction*. It was at this moment that Nirvana recorded and released their first single, "Love Buzz" / "Big Cheese." The eras of glam metal and grunge overlap, but the shift in rock's center of gravity, when it happens, is decisive.

The term *grunge* predates Nirvana as an adjective describing a developing sound in and around Seattle. Mark Arm, later of Seattle bands Green River and Mudhoney, used it descriptively as early as 1981, while Bruce Pavitt, founder of Nirvana's original SubPop record label, is credited with popularizing grunge as a genre name.[3] The emerging style's first definitive single came from a discussion between Arm and Pavitt.[4] This was "Touch Me I'm Sick," released in August 1988, which Britain's leading pop musical journal *NME* would name one of the "100 Greatest Singles of All Time."[5] Produced by Jack Endino, who would also produce *Bleach,* it's a blitz of breakneck self-loathing at the horizon of parody, and the better for it. Much of the feeling is carried in the almost impossibly fuzzy guitar sound, so distorted it's as if it can't bear to be itself. The lyrics are minimal: "I feel bad and I've felt worse," they begin after a few howls, "I'm a creep yeah I'm a jerk. Come on touch me I'm sick."

The song is a descendant of early metal's distorted blues stomps, and of seventies power punk. As guitarist Steve Turner put the matter, "In retrospect, it's The Yardbirds' 'Happenings Ten Years Time Ago' by way of the Stooges' 'Sick of You.'"[6] This is, in a slovenly schematic, grunge's hybrid heritage: metal and punk, relayed through the Melvins down to Soundgarden and Mudhoney, and modulated along the way by avant-rock acts such as Sonic Youth and the Pixies, and a mix of less apparent micro-influences. Such is the hybridized lineage from which Nirvana emerges; its ascendance would rescale the independent breakthrough of "Touch Me I'm Sick." When that song had its first success, recalls Mark Arm, "I said to the rest of the guys, 'Hang on, the rollercoaster ride is about to begin.' Turns out we were in the kiddie park."[7]

HERE ARE THREE CHORDS

Nirvana's rollercoaster ride had yet to begin when Cobain copied out the "Calvinist" (as was said of Johnson's followers) negative formula. If he was pushing back against the metallic lineage by way of testing exactly what grunge's inheritance might include, he was echoing the other main genealogical line by insisting on grunge as a kind of punk reformation. "Learn *not* to play your instrument" consciously lays claim to a 1976 invocation that became one of punk rock's formularies: a crude diagram and a few words in the British fanzine *Sideburns*. "THIS IS A CHORD," it reads in scrawl over a quick rendering of fingerings for an A, E, and G. "THIS IS ANOther. This IS A THIRD." And then the underscored conclusion: "NOW FORM A BAND."[8]

The imperative logic is straightforward enough: *Anyone can do it. Don't bow down before the band; be the band. Don't wait. Don't get stuck at home practicing scales. Raw power is enough. Urgency is enough. Anything more might just make things worse.*

This rhetoric of the amateur is historically ambivalent (and not simply because the punk/D.I.Y. community's real advances in inclusion, predictably enough, failed to dissolve imbalances of access and participation). Even if punk's rejection of technocratic specialization offers a romantic solidarity with manual labor, the gesture mirrors in part the deskilling of the work force. In the stagnating economy of seventies Great Britain, this becomes a problematic identification with wage rollbacks and Labour's "social contract." Nonetheless, the formulary is an early calculation of punk's social aesthetics. It preexists the more explicit social polemics that would follow (especially in the U.K.), which Jon Savage has eloquently argued come from Rock against Racism, "The organization that had inserted the Left discourse into Punk."[9]

The distinction is not so easy to draw as Savage suggests, however. *Sideburns's* diagram has a "Left discourse" and more kernelized within it, not polemical but material. Training and technique aren't purely technical barriers to entry; they bear the concealed ideological payloads of the moneyed middle class, of bourgeois dauphins with their home lessons and fab gear—barriers that implicitly do all the traditional work of exclusion along lines of class, race, gender.

The diagram, and the aesthetic form it commands, do not overtly express a political position. But neither do they offer a mere system of style (though one is never surprised when things end that way). Rather, the formulary takes part in the dialectical formation of politics and style, each giving definition and direction to the other. As we saw in chapter 1, the logic of amateurism, with its low-cost conversion of consumers to producers, has—regardless of express rhetorics—a political potential within it, as surely as it has a sound.

So it should surprise no one that the permissions of "NOW FORM A BAND" might provide purchase for Rock against Racism, that it might unfold into "White Riot" or "Boredom"—into the politics of punk's heroic era, which, while by no means monolithic, insistently opposed itself to economic and institutional power. This might take the form of critique (the kind of dogmatisms to which Savage points) or ragged negation (historically contextualized elsewhere).[10] In their gleefully excessive manners, each threatened dismissibility, be it the Sex Pistols' piss-taking or the Clash's lyrics to "1977": "In 1977, knives in West 11; ain't so lucky to be rich, Sten guns in Knightsbridge." These moments offered poses hard to credit with high moral seriousness, even if—especially if—one were more persuaded by the rigorous attacks of the Mekons and Gang of Four that would follow.

But then, it must have been hard to credit "Aristocrats to the lamp-posts!" as well, a doubt that falsifies neither the desire nor the following history. The desire, be it liberal or reactionary, to dismiss such demands never originates the lyrics themselves. If the Clash had only the Notting Hill Carnival Riot in place of revolution, the music was nonetheless an attempt to find a form adequate to its moment. The opposition was Enoch Powell, the National Front, and the Neo-Nazi movement; it was economic war on the council estates. It was bloated rock and old white farts. It was the boredom on offer, the "suss laws," the idiot spectacle of the Queen's Jubilee and the real conditions of Brixton.[11] In the famously less politicized U.S. punk scene, the fury turned more often toward the actual or imagined audience, toward the conditions of spectatorship and consumption: the Ramones' seventeen-minute shows; television's "Blank Generation"; confrontational stage shows that often enough leapt the stage into the crowd.

Confrontation itself coordinates all these disparate reaches of punk, for all their contingent and willed disorder. Confrontation is the order of the day. If certain political furies organize it here and there, it dwells also in the musical form, in the social imagination, in the structure of feeling. Confrontation is one of the secrets congealed within that most minimal imperative: "HERE ARE THREE CHORDS."

HOW MANY WAYS TO GET WHAT YOU WANT

Cobain's revisiting of that punk desideratum is, before anything else, a choice of one lineage over another, punk over metal. It stands as a kind of reformation—against the cyclical intensification of rock's professionalization and most immediately the slick trappings of glam metal. This resides in the phrase as surely as it does in his conversion narrative of seeing the Melvins in a parking lot: "When I saw them play, it just blew me away. I was instantly a punk rocker."[12]

This is already a somewhat wishful choice; punk rock and metal cleave too closely together for an either/or. They are the two forms of pop music most in elliptical orbit around antisociality—as a politics or a style, with punk drawn toward the former pole, metal the latter. American punk in particular passes its willful audience provocations down and across to later metal, or at least a strain of it; James Chance's audience-baiting "Natives Are Restless" returns as Gun N' Roses' "One in a Million," with homophobia added to the racism and misogyny. The latter act's *Appetite for Destruction* recalls Savage's epigraph for his pivotal chapter about the summer of 1976: Mikhail Bakunin's "The passion for destruction is also a creative passion!"[13] It remains the case that grunge's formal composition owes as much to metal as to punk. When *Nevermind* swept metal off the chart peaks, it was a more fratricidal moment than could be acknowledged at the time.

For all that, Cobain's impulse is evident enough as the election of an ethos, an affect, a history. Nothing secures this so clearly and schematically as the cultural sentiment captured in the title of David Markey's film *1991: The Year Punk Broke*. The title, as it happens, comes from an incidental counterposing of punk and metal. Markey, on tour with a number of punk, post-punk, and grunge bands on a European tour, finds himself watching television in a hotel room. "European MTV is showing Motley Crüe struggling through a version of the Sex Pistols' 'Anarchy in the UK' at some big European festival. Perhaps maybe one of the ones we'll be at. Can jetlag cause you to hallucinate something this surreal? I make a sarcastic comment, 'Wow, 1991 is the year that punk rock finally breaks.'"[14]

Markey's sarcasm, and the film's title, depends on recognizing that the bands with which he travels are the real punks. The documentary was initially designed to feature Sonic Youth, the traveling cast's elders alongside the Ramones, both dating to the seventies. Sonic Youth had the previous year released *Goo,* their first album on a major label. Nirvana signed in turn with the same label, Geffen, urged on by Sonic Youth's Kim Gordon. As it plays out, the tour coincides with the dawn of Nirvana's international stardom; their charismatic whirlpool grows more irresistible show by show, and this hijacks the story. By the end of the year, *Nevermind* is selling 400,000 records a week.[15] By the time the film is released, it seems to be about them.

The spirit of the film, and of the cultural ferment from which it arises, is one of celebratory (if chaotic) continuity. There is little sense of intergenerational conflict or resentment, but rather—as the title captures—a feeling that long-standing struggles have come to fruition. Marginalized and embattled punk had finally realized its popular authority, in the form of grunge.

It's against this local history that grunge's emergence as a cultural phenomenon must be measured. If it is at once reformation, continuation, and realization, it also takes on crucial differences. "Learn *not* to play your instrument," as a recurrence of "HERE ARE THREE CHORDS," certainly bears the original's political traces. But the slogan cannot finally have the same valences as its source.

The distance between the two formulations is determined greatly by what has passed between them, between 1976 and 1989. The earlier conceives of starting from zero, offers the minimal necessary lesson. By the later version, a blank slate is no longer part of the imagination; *unlearning* will be required. The suspicion that naiveté is a lost position, or one that was always delusory, has won the day. It will take actual work to expunge technical habits and ideological hobgoblins. Intervening developments that arrange this changed perspective include such things as second-wave feminism and other new social movement rhetorics, as well as a growing sense of rock's own belatedness. One can no longer stare forward at the future, the opposition, the possible. A part of consciousness is already up ahead and looking back at naive commitments, a withering Orphic glance that takes the form of irony.

I DON'T WANNA, I DON'T THINK SO

This shift in self-awareness is captured by Sonic Youth, the film's transitional figure (appropriately enough, as they're a musicologically transitional figure between punk and grunge as well, in parallel to their progressive synthesis of free and out jazz, avant-garde minimalism and other more highbrow and experimental tendencies). Tied to New York's knowing downtown intelligentsia, they're a band in which the social antagonisms of punk are preserved and ironized at once. Their most successful single, 1990's "Kool Thing," dates from the moment in which grunge is at once consolidating punk's furies while shifting their vector. Over a buzzy guitar that straddles the two genres, Kim Gordon exits the minimal melody for a spoken interlude reminiscent of Patti Smith. "Kool thing," she wonders with her affected lack of affect, " . . . what are you gonna do for me? I mean, are you gonna liberate us girls from male white corporate oppression?" Public Enemy's Chuck D (rejoining us from chapter 1) exhorts her, "Tell it like it is. Yeah."

This droll residue of "Left discourse," and its imbricated political others, is what grunge will finally abandon. Not every punk-inspired idiom of the era

Figure 8. Kool Things: Sonic Youth in 1990, the droll residue of punk. (Video dir. Tamra Davis, DGC Records)

took this same turn. Tobi Vail, who passed the fated slogan on to Kurt, would take part in the refashioning and revitalizing of punk's oppositional politics that happened in bands like Bikini Kill, Bratmobile, and other groups under the banner of "riot grrrl"—a phrase sometimes credited to Vail. The movement's motto was REVOLUTION GIRL STYLE NOW. But this is exactly why riot grrrl was not grunge, but something else (and, arguably, why it couldn't achieve similar levels of success even if it wished to).[16] Grunge constituted itself by doing a very specific thing with punk's will to confrontation: turning it inward.

Another way to pose this issue is to note that the most basic difference between the language of "NOW FORM A BAND" and "Learn *not* to play your instrument" will turn out to be the most decisive. If both demands are in the second person, one is addressed plurally, and the other singularly. Even more suggestively, it's clear enough that the former is projected outward, an urgent and even confrontational challenge to anyone who might encounter it. Even the seemingly reversed position of Richard Hell's famous t-shirt with a painted target labeled "Please Kill Me" (this is a world made entirely of imperatives) is scarcely introspective. "People had some wild ideas back then," recounts the photographer Bob Gruen, "but for somebody to walk the streets of New York with a target on his chest, with an invitation to be killed—that's quite a statement."[17] It doesn't waver from punk's confrontations; it simply reverses the telescope, which inevitably turns out to be a gun sight.

"Learn *not* to play your instrument," in Cobain's notebook, has the force of an admonition to the mirror. It becomes immediately part of his ulcerous self-doubt, dovetailing with Mudhoney's hyperbolic self-loathing in sound and sensibility. The motion from one of these stances to the other is central to, and inextricable from, grunge's way of being. Among many modes, this inward turn is *the* mode.

I DON'T BELONG HERE

Cobain's self-doubt, even self-contempt, is everywhere inescapable; it lodges in his clotted howl whether he's forming words or not, and even when he assays a love song. But the sensation is not just in the sound: "I need an easy friend," begins the band's first great tune, as if he's already abandoned any standards and hates himself for it. This is the indelible "About a Girl"; its sweet nothings only get worse from there. "I'll take advantage while you hang me out to dry," he announces, not particularly surprised at either party's failings. No outside world intrudes on the song's resentful, obsessive romance; it's not a room with a view. Even in this catchy, inviting melody (reputedly written after a day of listening to the Beatles), the scene is stained. It spreads across the entire 1989 debut, *Bleach,* and Cobain knows it. "Is there another reason for your stain?" begins the chorus of the opener, "Blew." This stain is not remarkably ambiguous; the chorus ends, "Here is another word that rhymes with *shaaaamme!*" The refrain of "Floyd the Barber," one of multiple songs to dabble in disgust about the body, is nothing but "I'm ashamed" (or "I was ashamed") repeated thrice, the final vowel drawn out again.

Doubt, fixation, resentful need, self-loathing, shame. This is the elixir: profoundly angry introspection. One of Nirvana's triumphs is to find a sound for this, unsettling, immiserated, but at the same time immensely agitated. It's punk rock turned outside in, not *anti-social* but *a-social.* For punk's antagonistics, an agonized self; for outward confrontation, immiserated retreat. For negation, sheer negativity. The surrealistically morphing image sequences that will become a lyrical mainspring also convey the deformations of an interior landscape: "And the car, twist, mouth, fear, yeaaah!" yells Cobain in the metal sludge of "Paper Cuts." Later: "My whole existence is for your fears." It's a wonder there can be a *you* at all; it is no one outside his head.

For a moment of disgusted litany in "Downer," the dissatisfaction with social engagement becomes explicit: "Sickening pessimists, picketing masses, separated communists, apocalyptic bastards." Farewell to all of that. Cobain was unhesitating about the music's psychologized nature: "The early songs were really angry. But as time goes on the songs are getting poppier and poppier as I get happier and happier. The songs are now about conflicts in relationships, emotional things with other human beings." To which he added, "Sometimes I try to make things harder for myself, just to try to make myself a little more angry."[18] One trusts his claims about happiness are driven in part by a guilty need to explain the band's popularity along some other axis than that of commercial accommodation. Regardless, this location of the source of grunge's furies—entirely attuned to the personal rather than the social—is telling enough. In the album's most traditionally punk-styled track, "Negative Creep," a brief flicker of social rage immediately makes the inward turn: "I'm a negative creep!" whines Cobain upward of a dozen times. At first this is followed by " . . . and I'm stoned," a phrase shortly replaced with a wordless moan.

If "shame" is the keyword that won't dissolve in *Bleach,* "creep" is the keyword that survives grunge's duration. "Negative Creep" stands between Mudhoney's 1988 "I'm a creep yeah I'm a jerk" and, in the last days of grunge, Stone Temple Pilots' "Creep" and Radiohead's first hit, also called "Creep." That Radiohead didn't turn out to be a grunge act at all only proves the point. Later, Thom Yorke would direct his spectral falsetto toward more aestheticized abstractions better conjoined with the band's longueurs, most famously in the dystopian fantasia of *OK Computer.* But in 1993, Radiohead was compelled to fit itself into grunge's mold, enough so that they would be derided as "Nirvana-lite."[19] And it was clear how this could be done: "I'm a creep, I'm a weirdo," sang Yorke, echoing Mark Arm almost exactly.[20]

This then is *Bleach*'s position: at the corner of *creep* and *shame.* The coordination of these two is the first brute truth of grunge as an achieved structure of feeling: the unceasing and unstable encounter with one's own undesirability, one's own failings, one's unsuccessfully hidden or managed aberrations. This may be grunge's last truth as well—that which, once lost, leaves nothing behind.

Nevermind was mostly composed in 1989 and 1990, and released in 1991—the High Grunge era. It realized the initial impulses of its genre as totally as anything on record. Its stylistic differences from *Bleach* might be reduced as such: *Nevermind* is more melodically complex and influenced by the pop tradition, the songs are more likely to have dynamic shifts in tempo and mood, and the lyrics are more extensive, oblique and allusive. The playing is better. The album is more expensively produced and sounds bigger, louder; even its plaintiveness is overwhelming. But its monumentality in the rearview mirror doesn't offer a sufficient explanation of its unforeseen success: Geffen hoped to sell 250,000 copies, and as of 2007 was well past 25 million. The question of what exactly allowed *Nevermind* to surmount both Guns N' Roses and Michael Jackson—seemingly to banish such music to the outer dark—remains unanswered and perhaps unanswerable, though such matters are near the heart of this book.

The album's oldest song, "Polly," is built from a specific act of abjection: the identification with a kidnapper-rapist. There are many versions of the song, with variations among then; the lineaments stay the same. The first-person narration gets more awful with each brief phrase: "Polly wants a cracker; think I should get off her first. Think she wants some water—to put out the blow torch." Disavowal follows swiftly, in the form of the chorus: "Isn't me, have a seat." This is not a sundering of the identification between singer and character, the storyteller stepping out of the story; it's the rapist futilely trying to flee from himself. The telegraphic fragments are only horrific: "Let me clip, dirty wings, let me take a ride, cut yourself, want some help, please myself, got some rope." The song takes place in a threatening double confinement: within the imagined suburban dungeon and the captor's fissured psyche. The world at large—social existence—is, more than ever, lacking any real substance; it's beyond thought. No one escapes from the song.

The doubled interiority of "Polly" still has a whiff of the outside; there is at least another body in the room (albeit suffering), one who desires to leave, to return to the world. "Lithium," signally, offers nothing of the sort. "I'm so happy 'cause today I've found my friends," Cobain sings with a forced smile of a croon over a loping progression, bass-heavy but open. "They're in my head." This is the arena exactly; it is not the only time the album presents "friends" who swiftly turn out to be mental phantoms. They're a substitute for actual contact, which is itself too risky: "I'm so horny but that's okay my will is good." The story, we gather, could turn into "Polly" at any moment. As the band makes its turn toward the chorus—every track instantly doubled, trebled, distorted toward chaos—Cobain does nothing but howl "yeah" with varying, tortuous emphases. Never has a *Yes* so utterly meant *No*. Eventually he arrives at the song's desperate claim: "I like it, I'm not gonna crack. I miss you, I'm not gonna crack. I love you, I'm not gonna crack." And then, finally, "I kill you. I'm not gonna crack." No one believes it. No one overlooks the fact that the music has cracked already. This offers the genre's version of literary irony—Sonic Youth's social ironizing turned entirely back on itself. There is no other to be doubted before the self.

The affects and sensations that overflow the album are more or less those of *Bleach,* amplified. Shame competes with guilt; bodily disgust yields pride of place to sexual violence; self-loathing still dominates, redoubled with every failure of control. Though the balances and tonalities are different, the structure of feeling is continuous with the debut album. What has changed is the music's formal sophistication. The dynamic attack from verse to chorus—gaining in tempo, volume, density—becomes the band's signal device. As a song structure it's taken largely from the Pixies and given an emotional coherence, more forceful and more rhetorically pointed. It becomes the genre's defining form exactly because it captures the instability found within the genre's defining tension between the introspection of the singer-songwriter and the rages of early rock, metal, and punk. It doesn't offer a synthesis but an oscillation. The contradiction isn't finally resolvable, which is exactly the problem: it is not a dynamic that can come to rest, either emotionally or formally.

"Lithium" serves as the dynamic's Rosetta stone, though the form should not be reduced to a simple analogy for bipolar disorder, as critics of a biographical stripe have been inclined to do. The verse, certainly marked as depressive, is more rightly defined by the doomed attempt to maintain self-control through various means. The chorus is the sound of the psyche breaking the restraints of will and pharmacology: not just mania, but terror over what might happen next. Thus it is inevitable that this escape does not open out into the world; its abandon drives deeper still into the mind. In the classic Nirvana song, the alternation is between two internments: that of impossible self-control, and that of retreat into furious madness.

The dynamic's apotheosis is doubtless "Smells Like Teen Spirit," the album's lead single with which grunge traversed the line from subculture to mainstream. In true emergent style, it first appeared as a novelty song: even as the video entered heavy rotation on MTV, newly added subtitles rendered comedic Cobain's half-choate howlings. The verse is built on a simple rhythm pattern counterpointed by a repeated pair of ringing guitar notes. Like "Lithium," a fictive "little group" swiftly diminishes: "It's fun to lose and to pretend." At the edge of the chorus, nobody is there. "Hello hello hello," he inquires of the abyss, "how low?"

Cobain's pervasive device of repeating a word with slipping shifts of inflection to reach an ironic homonym is a deep link to the punk tradition. Surely Cobain borrowed it from Johnny Rotten's axiomatic "I am an Antichrist, I am an anarchist." The difference between Rotten and Cobain could not be more stark, however. In the later moment, anarchy is loosed not upon the world, but the psyche. There is no world, no U.K., no U.S.A. By the chorus, "Teen Spirit" has diminished to a lone figure worrying the mysterious sequence "a mulatto, an albino, a mosquito, my libido," the sense of this floating as remote as the singer. The sound is a maelstrom. And then, finally, "Polly"'s disavowal returns without even someone to do the disavowing, just a pure concept languishing in inner space as the song chants down to zero: "A denial, a denial, a denial. . . ." This limns exactly the distinction between negation and negativity. The homemade assault on the ego is absolute. Here one can see the corollary rationale for jettisoning traditional guitar heroics: not just a rejection of technocratic, masculinist professionalism, but a refusal of the solo's egotism in favor of self-abnegation.[21]

On an album where phrase after phrase is exemplary, iconic, it's difficult to precipitate out the most suggestive. A good candidate, however, would be "Teen Spirit"'s "I feel stupid and contagious." This last offers a folded account of grunge's turn away from social engagement, away from social space itself. To the situation presented in *Bleach*, *Nevermind* proposes the only possible solution: quarantine. "I'm on a plain," runs the song also called "On a Plain." "I can't complain. I'm on a plain." For all its seeming openness, this is the psychic landscape of quarantine, of overdetermined inwardness, sequestered inside a disordered mind that is inside a body in turn removed from the public sphere.

THE PICTURES HAVE ALL BEEN WASHED IN BLACK

In the real public world, the tension between the genre's ethos and its inconceivable economic and cultural success had already doomed grunge by 1991. This Malthusian authenticity trap threatens any art that launches its appeals or critiques from the margins of the excluded, the reviled. The sense of vindication with which grunge "broke" punk from the confines of subculturality into the core of popular culture was short-lived, and had been irresolvably contradictory from the start; the genre's continuity with punk, incomplete as it was, still sufficed to render success as failure. The inward turn could no more coexist with Marc Jacobs's grunge *couture* show in the fall of 1992 than could the Mekons' bracing *Kapitalkritik*.[22] The difficult knowledge that Nirvana and company had ambivalently solicited such success only sharpened the trap's silver jaws.

Cobain's 1994 suicide was punctuation. The band's 1993 *In Utero,* desperately abrasive and monstrous in tandem with a hermetic surrealism, made apparent by its popularity that grunge had forfeited the capacity either to repel or retreat. The album's title, with its pathos-laden wish image of primal interiority, was clear enough; lead single "Heart Shaped Box" pressed the ambivalent fascination with supernal enclosure clearer still, while linking itself to the initial success-disaster of "Teen Spirit" by taking that song's signal bent guitar note as the vocal device that begins the chorus of "Box." But there was no way out, including going further in. The grimly beautiful ballad "All Apologies" admits this with its title, while the lyric itself becomes a catalog of Cobain's tropes: "Married, buried," he repeats. Focusing the song's messianic beam, he offers, "I'll take all the blame," before returning to his original keyword, now rendered cinematic and dreamy: "aqua seafoam shame." Inescapably, the shame now included the genre's fate, and having wanted it. Released four weeks later, Pearl Jam's album *Vs.* set a single-week record for a disc of any kind, selling just shy of one million copies.[23]

Forever T. S. Eliot to Nirvana's Ezra Pound, Pearl Jam was burdened with the unannounced (and surely unintended) task of opening grunge to a still-broader audience—an effect achieved through the subtraction of bodily disgust and explicit sexual violence as well as a smoothing of the guitar attack (in a way oddly redolent of classic rock and even the glam metal that grunge had overthrown).

It is perhaps inevitable that the consequence of these tweaks to the formula would be a slight return toward social thematic. The imagined subject of Pearl Jam songs is less a threat in need of quarantine; the technically nimble music doesn't promise to crack open at every moment. Nonetheless, grunge's characteristic introspection remains. "Alive," their debut single, specifies the problem as survivor's guilt—a canny figuring of grunge's signature affect and isolation. "You're still alive, she said. Oh, and do I deserve to be? Is that the question? And if so: who answers . . . who answers . . . ?" In a by now familiar sequence, guilt and self-doubt (here flattered to be a portentous existential cry) proceed to remove the scene and singer from human interaction until the chamber is empty and echoing. The song's closing erasure endures as the band's preferred trope: "The pictures have all been washed in black," as one lugubrious ballad concludes. Another single from the first album, "Jeremy," involves the guttural descent into the mind of a traumatically disturbed schoolboy. The song is pointedly psychologized, particularly around pop-Oedipal suggestions. The music video suggests that the story ends in a schoolroom massacre as the boy lashes back at tormentors real or imagined. But the lyric—per grunge's habit—never arrives at this moment in which socially dangerous rage is unleashed outward.

There is surely a breadth of possible forms that interior psychodrama can take, and various effacements of the social. Some combination of the two, one comes to understand, will be required to perform the genre, in addition to awkwardly replicable sonic devices. In retrospect, the sharp edges of the genre's historical demarcation are striking. Pearl Jam, for example, tellingly revisited the punk tradition of social engagement almost immediately after Cobain's suicide, adopting an escalating social-political rhetoric inaugurated with 1994's *Vitalogy*. The sonic and lyrical peregrinations of Pearl Jam are perhaps more symptomatic than those of their betters; not the best of grunge, they're in some wise the most schematically revealing. This is the fate of the band that comes second; in point of fact, they are the first band to follow the rules as rules, to register them as that which constellates a genre.[24] The inward turn and its accompanying structure of feeling seem organic to Nirvana, an invention that couldn't be uninvented; Pearl Jam, contrarily, pursues these sensations as a choice, against competing impulses, only for as long as the genre's center holds.

C'MON, LOVE ONE ANOTHER RIGHT NOW

The matter at hand is that of difference. Representation, analogy, allegory won't do. In attempting to understand grunge's apparition on the cultural stage at just this moment and no other—and its popularity, its influence—it would be a mistake to settle for the claim that it simply provided a set of feelings appropriate for the experience of the era. Nor can its aesthetic qualities by themselves prove a positive account of the moment's form, be the sign of the times—a formal allegory, the sound of a wall being knocked down. Pop music loves such allegories—but part of what it loves is the very incompleteness and seductive superficiality of such an account. Nonetheless, these are the kind of analyses favored by a popular strain of cultural studies in the United States, and though they can be eloquent about synchronic relationships, they are not always as attentive to diachronic developments, to change.

That axis, of course, is not sufficient either: to say that grunge is not punk, even to specify how, does not an historical argument make. Why grunge had to make *that* change, *then*—this is the minimum. This is the question of emergence: What did grunge have to abandon to become what it was, and what were the contours of that change? This is the difference that matters in beginning to think historical change.

It's this difference toward which the "inward turn" gestures. It can only be understood *as a turn* in relation to the already existing vectors of its line, its lineage. In part by its own election, this overarching lineage is punk rock. Grunge's inward turn is exactly that turn away from punk's social confrontation. "Let fury have the hour, anger can be power," sang Joe Strummer— another punk axiom. For grunge, with its belatedness, the fury would be preserved as both power and danger, as a threatening release that must be turned away from the world to do its destructive work in the interior of the disintegrating psyche. It is an emergence that for all the world looks, ironically, like submersion.[25] Thus it signally becomes a psychologized rather than socialized musical adventure. At the same time, it would be a solecism to suggest that a phenomenon so popular has no social meaning; rather, its social meaning is the turn from the social.

Nor is that the sum of irony. Indeed, grunge offers irony with a vengeance. Its inward turn, and the dynamic pivot that defines Nirvana's song structure, might both be grasped as formal ironies: as the form turning to look back at the content and, in so doing, undoing it.

This is not proposed as a failure—grunge as punk minus its political ambitions, a self-absorbed diminution. To so believe would be to miss the point almost entirely. Like any persuasive art, grunge could only hope to be *of its time* and not another. Its attunement to its moment, to 1989, is exactly what's at stake here, and any attunement would be impossible without both preservation of, and a turning from, its lineage. *It must change,* as the poet said. The undoing is part of this.

Nowhere is the undoing of political pretensions more evident than in the opening moments of *Nevermind*'s "Territorial Pissings," when bassist Krist Novoselic obliterates the Youngbloods' 1967 nadir, "Get Together." "C'mon, people now, smile on your brother . . . ," he begins, then dismisses the chorus in a single breathless, tuneless shriek in which, as Greil Marcus observes, "you can hear unmitigated contempt for this project, along with a gleeful realization of how stupid it is."[26] But something is wrong here. This scornful rejection does not belong to grunge at all. It is two turns back, at least.

And so we see, in a single gesture, the continuity and the rupture both present in 1989. It was one of punk's historical missions to negate the moon-eyed social dream of sixties pop. Grunge, with no intention of recalling such idealisms after the fashion of rave's Second Summer of Love, nonetheless negates the negation of punk. This spirit of the Summer of Love is the sixties ploughshare that punk had already beaten into a sword, which in turn is the sword that grunge turned on itself.

Just a Stop Down the Line

Grunge's inward turn is replicated beyond the confines of the genre, most evidently in the adjacent but more capacious arena of "modern rock" (into which grunge and "alternative rock" would shortly be folded). When grunge arrived, U2 had nearly a decade of hypertrophied success on the books; it remains striking that their finest album (by a considerable measure) was released in 1991, openly influenced by both grunge and electronic dance music. Both of these emergent genres left sonic traces and donated some elements of their structures of feeling, but the former more decisively infected the album's emotional tenor. From the title on, *Achtung Baby* evinces a degree of irony distinct from the band's earnest tradition; among other things, the disc announced U2's period of autocritique, with its accompanying send-ups of rock stardom (itself redolent of the KLF's contemporaneous delights, albeit without the crooked grins and explicit capitalist critique).[1] Overfuzzed guitars and distorted vocals orchestrated much the same self-disgust that grunge had codified; Bono seemed, for the first time, at odds with himself more than with the world. Largely absent were the band's familiar calls to spiritual, social, and political engagement and confrontation.[2] A half-dozen singles, each one ambivalently erotic/romantic and variously haunted by self-doubt, dominated the Modern Rock charts in late 1991 and on into 1992.[3]

The album was not without social resonance. *Achtung Baby*'s most suggestive and finally most renowned song is "One," in no small part because of the multiple video clips released to promote it. While the title offers a flatfooted monosyllabic return to the theme of unity, the more nimble videos in many regards confirm "One" as a song of queer pathos, insisting plaintively on gay love as equal but not identical to other loves. Much of the proceeds from singles sales went to AIDS-related charities. One video takes images from gay artist/activist David Wojnarowicz, while another features the band in drag as Bono sings to his father.

The latter video (directed by Anton Corbijn) is set in Berlin and cut with shots of the Wall, Brandenburg Gate, and the band driving Trabants through the streets of Berlin, where the song, indeed much of the album, was recorded—band and crew having arrived on October 3, 1990, the day of reunification. The glam drag in turn summons the Berlin of Bowie and *Cabaret;* it also follows by a year the Nirvana video for "In Bloom," in which that band appears in dresses.[4] Meanwhile, the album's opening track, "Zoo Station," is named for Berlin's busy subway and train station (as is Scorpions' 1980 song "The Zoo"). *Bahnhof Berlin Zoologischer Garten* had been West Berlin's central hub while the Wall stood, and the only point at which one could take a train from West to East (and back by midnight if one had only a day pass): a transfer station.

This offers a broad figure for *Achtung Baby,* which served as a transfer wherein the energies of recently emergent genres could move into a more generalized pop sphere. But the album produces a more specific exchange: it's a document of the era located at the transfer between grunge's inward turn and the external situation of Berlin, the end of the Cold War and the Fall of the Wall. It is perhaps merely poetic that another of the album's opaque, ambivalent love songs bears the improbably Fukuyaman title, "Until the End of the World."

CHAPTER 4

The Billboard Consensus

THE PERIOD AROUND 1989 saw the greatest run of pop hits since 1962, that belle époque of the single before the ascent of the Beatles and the rule of the album.

There can be no evidence for this claim. What can be argued is that pop music, not a genre itself and thus ineligible for emergence in the sense we've been using, can nonetheless be a sign of the times. As the tautologically dominant, indexed directly to popularity (and thus to economics' final determining instance), it is still positioned to register changes in the psychic life of shared culture.[1] Such registrations, however, happen perforce less precipitously than in individual genres; it's called "mass culture" for a reason, and the current of the mainstream is slower to divert than the Alpheus and Peneus.

Some material facts obtain, certainly. The year 1989 saw the first number one single not to be released on vinyl. The conversion from analog to easily programmable digital formats would turn out to be a shift favoring the individual song over the record. The period turned out to be a kind of belle époque for the *measure* of pop itself—a process that changed irrevocably in November 1991, when *Billboard*'s method of generating the Hot 100 (and all other charts) converted from a quasi-empirical phone survey to the Nielsen SoundScan, which collates data from cash registers across the nation.

The problem of making the Hot 100 speak is in some degree the problem of this book *in nuce*. Conjoined by a capacity to reach across genre lines (and often excoriated for a corresponding blandness, by those with discriminating sensibilities), pop hits might be understood as pregeneric, lacking sufficient identifying marks to place themselves certainly within an established genre. At the same time, pop in its metageneric quality fills its rolls from a breadth of genres.[2]

This presents certain difficulties. Not only can there be no generic emergence within pop, no real struggle over its character beyond a preference expressed in dollars, but the term itself is fundamentally unstable. Scarcely a song is mentioned in this study that *isn't* pop in the market sense; nonetheless, this chapter pursues a period sensibility as if there were a semi-independent category, *pop as pop*. This must indeed be part of the argument: that in their very deracination, the songs were after something they couldn't otherwise reach. That said, various of the songs over which this chapter pauses might reasonably appear elsewhere. A song on the Hot 100 is likely to appear as well on another more specific chart: Modern Rock, or 12″ Sales, or Hot R&B/Hip-Hop Songs. Such is the great paradox of the Hot 100, and of Top 40 radio; agreed by a large phalanx of serious music fans to be homogenous in nature, it boasts nonetheless a high degree of stylistic variation in comparison to most programmed single-genre formats.

There is a further way to pose the paradox of pop music and the problem of historical characterization. As one critic phrased things, "[Pop] songs seem to have no historical markers because they're perfectly time-bound; 'timeless' is so similar to the surrounding atmosphere that hearing it is like having no experience at all. Or maybe like sitting in a warm bathtub drinking a glass of water. 'Pop' is sort of another name for 'room temperature.'"[3]

How, then, to characterize this latter pop belle époque lacking for avowed politics or native soil, without local habits or genre determinations, without any cultural grounds but the abstraction of culture itself? This question, finally, is less desperate than it might seem, for if pop bets everything on being timeless, that itself is a historical wager.

WHAT ELSE DO I HAVE TO SAY

If pop is limited in its historical grasp, the desire for it to attempt something of the sort is not altogether lacking. Billy Joel's "We Didn't Start the Fire," with its four decades of textbook citation, is scarcely the only song to offer a historical assay. Among precursors, its increasingly breathless list instantly recalls R.E.M.'s single from two years before, "It's the End of the World as

We Know It (and I Feel Fine)." This earlier song is more impressionistic and obscure, mustering an ambiguous apocalypticism; in 1987, one can see the desire called history coming into view, but not into focus.

Joel's list—119 newsworthy characters and events from 1949 to 1989 before a final interjection—marches past in one-year lyrical units, with occasional pauses for the chorus, until a sudden sprint for the finish (leaping from 1964 to the present over the course of twenty-five seconds). It starts in 1949, the year of Joel's birth and one year after the Berlin Blockade. Popular music and the Cold War are easily the best-represented topics: the former gets roughly sixteen mentions, the latter more than thirty, from "Red China" (1949) through "China's under martial law" (1989), not neglecting "Berlin" (1961) and of course "Communist bloc," bound to rhyme with "Rock around the Clock." Figure and ground, gradually leveling. The elision of pop and geopolitics is neatly underscored in the final entry, "rock 'n' roller cola wars."[4]

"In musical terms," according to critic Hua Hsu, the song is "objectively terrible."[5] Doubtless sincere, such a claim proposes an extraordinary quality where there is none. *Content content hook:* relentless, repetitive, conjuring variation largely through tone of voice, "We Didn't Start the Fire" resembles much pop music, only more so—an exception only in that it does what hit songs do, but too much. Its reception, a classic calculus wherein popularity is inversely proportional to critical response (named one of the "50 Worst Songs Ever"), is again not an exception but a paradigm of pop.[6] Indeed, the song is exemplary in almost every regard.

But even the most exemplary pop must have, as part of its exemplarity, something that attaches it to its moment, a *particular unparticularity* that is the less dismissive analog to Adorno's "one feature by which it can be distinguished." It must have a way of universalizing itself which cannot itself be universal.

Part of the song's success, obviously, is contingent: "We Didn't Start the Fire" was released to radio in October in advance of *Storm Front,* the album released in turn on November 10, 1989—one day after the opening of the partition between East and West Germany.[7] Thus, that event cannot be mentioned in the song; the Fall of the Wall instead supplied the missing period to the song's endless sentence, with the song providing a way of participating in the magic of the moment.

But the song has a constructed appeal as well, an affect not at all responsive to a given event but still perfectly attuned to the moment, produced almost entirely through inflection and through the form's failure at song's close. Before that passage, the parade is steady. The Hungarian Revolution, the polio vaccine, Chubby Checker—all have a machined equivalence; the song remains unable to have an opinion about any particular thing. The song, does, however, have a clear feeling about the ceaseless, tumbling accretion of things as such: increasingly agitated, ascending in vocal pitch, and finally ending in the a cappella yelp, "I can't take it anymore!" In point of fact, he can take it just enough to revisit the chorus, with only a slight variation: "We didn't start the fire, it was always burnin' since the world's been turnin'; we didn't start the fire, but when we are gone it'll still burn on and on and on."

The desire called history is met by the problem of same: not what happens, not the perfectly flattened and equivalent instants, but their ceaseless cascade, driven by forces that are at once unchanging and always beyond reach. "We" are not the authors of what happens; by the end, we can't even manage the material through the auspices of narrative. Things fall apart.

This experience of immutable endlessness, of exploded time and a superfluity of history in the face of which meaningful action is impossible—this is the secret sense of the period in pop music. A feeling, if not a structure. Rarely is it phrased as a specifically historical problem, and this is only to be expected: because the historical dynamic is ungraspable, the affect must be grasped as a seemingly independent thing. It is a feeling felt sometimes as infinitude, sometimes apocalypse; sometimes perfect indifference, and sometimes liberation.

WHAT YOU GET FOR CHANGING YOUR MIND

George Michael's "Freedom '90" does not, of course, concern world events; its providential name was required to distinguish itself from the earlier Wham! song "Freedom." It nonetheless manages to crystallize the feeling of the post-Wall moment without taking a stance regarding it, through its sense of unbounded duration as liberation, its formal evocation of the sudden absence of barriers—and its sense of this as something potentially intrinsic to the music, to the truth of pop.

The lyrical niceties of the song are not hard to parse. As commercial autobiography, its opening gesture summons the familiar conversion from seeming to reality: the maturation from contrived pop star to real artist. In Michael's case, this clichéd story of integrity found must ghost for his gradual and more problematic self-revelation as a gay man, after having acceded to being marketed as "every little hungry schoolgirl's pride and joy." The lyrics work this double-shift with charming concision, including strategically ambiguous cliché ("sometimes the clothes do not make the man" and so forth) and

Figure 9. Supermodel surplus: George Michael, "Freedom '90." (Video dir. David Fincher, Epic Records)

directness ("when you shake your ass they notice fast; some mistakes were built to last").

The limits of this narrative are shaken by an irreconcilable vector: the song's unabashed pleasure in the very pop it claims to have exposed and outgrown. This happens transparently if surprisingly in the lyrics: "Heaven knows we sure had some fun boy, what a kick just a buddy and me," he sings, referring to his supposedly abject days in the germ-free duo Wham! "We had every big shot good-time band on the run boy, we were living in a fantasy." That this delight is casually tied to a male-male bond—that is, to the confessional's half-hidden truth—is one of the secrets the song yields. It shortly finds a place in the song's larger irony, wherein the main thrust of the lyrics is contradicted by the structure and melody.

At six and a half minutes, "Freedom '90" is an anomalous length for any pop song, much less one that spent forty weeks in the Hot 100. And yet its length does not turn out to be an occasion to vanquish the superficial felicities of the three-minute song; indeed, it has little interest in outgrowing the category of "pop." As a musical construction, the song goes about the very opposite: it's machined to appeal as broadly as possible, from its shuffle-beat and handclaps to its gospel chorus and series of major-key resolves.

The salient quality of "Freedom '90" is thus its very excess of hooks. Everything about the song speaks of this surfeit, from its sheer length, to the simultaneous presence of not one but several globally famous fashion models in the video, to the brand new vocal melody improvised around the chord structure during the closing fade—as if to suggest infinite invention, limited only arbitrarily and for the moment. This pleasurable excess is the song's logic. Against the masculine-coded renunciation of pleasure that historically defines the "mature" rejection of pop (which is for women and children), the song poses the truth of pleasure as the excess within pop—a rhetoric less than opaque regarding the song's shadow narrative of queer sexuality as unrecuperable excess and freedom at once.

The song finally proposes not freedom *from*, but freedom *through*. If it is transcendent—and it certainly feels that way—it does not seek to transcend pop but simply to explode bounded pop for the unbounded, without prohibition or border.

NO END AND NO BEGINNING

This sense of surfeit, this overflowing of borders, is another assay of pop music's condition around 1989 and after: it is exactly the way in which the pop of this moment is *too much pop* that orchestrates a belle époque. "Freedom '90," resisting the baroque despite its welter of melodic parts, insists on pop's possibilities for liberatory excess. In this regard it is preceded by Madonna's "Like a Prayer," released on the last day of February 1989.[8] Like Michael's song, "Like a Prayer" seems bent on exploding its category without exiting it: "as close to art as pop music gets."[9]

Such a judgment is inseparable from another periodizing development: it is around this moment that popular culture, and pop music in particular, becomes an object of increasingly serious scholarly attention—a change so thoroughly mediated by a single cultural figure that one scholar describes the "institutionalization of a major subdivision of American media studies into Madonna studies."[10] While this is in part a marker of Madonna's phenomenal appeal, it indexes as well pop's capacity to appear as the measure of the moment.

In a manner by now recognizable, the moment is measured by its exceeding of the momentary. Appearing briefly within the lyrics of "Like a Prayer," such transcendence risks becoming a thematic banality; it is rescued by the song's proliferation of melodic and rhythmic parts, so intensively elaborated over nearly six minutes that the passage of time does indeed seem compelled by the music rather than vice versa. The gospel choir presides not over the song's posed spirituality but, as in Michael, over the church of pop, and specifically pop's jubilant triumph over time. It feels like flying; mark that. This is pop's heaven, exactly as its hell is time out of joint, intuited in the FM revelations of the 1990 hit "Way Down Now" ("The clocks will all run backwards, all the sheep will have two heads, and Thursday night and Friday will be on Tuesday night instead").[11]

From either perspective, we are presented with the collapse of temporality, the end of narrative. It could scarcely be a surprise that the most celebratory versions of this feeling belong to the social quarters associated with the feminine, the queer, the childlike—regions with their own reasons for mistrusting linear time. However, such accounts of pop-as-resistance risk being a bit *too* Madonna Studies; as we have already come to suspect, the story of the end of stories has its own reasons to dominate the discourse after 1989. Pop's capturing of this affective whirl is equally its way of being of its time, of relaying the dominant story.

Moreover, it is easy to neglect the strand of melancholy that twines through the song, frays around the edges of Madonna's voice, the careful minor chord that comes forward insistently in the bridge, the song's uncertainty, *like, like, like,* the distant doubt as to whether this might in fact all be a dream.

YOU BETTER HAVE SOME FUN NO MATTER WHAT YOU DO

The mournful ballad "Nothing Compares 2 U" was composed around 1985 by Prince, making it an unlikely candidate to bear the impress of another time. Sinéad O'Connor's version five years later spent a full month at the top of the Hot 100, equaling the year's best chart performance and eventually winning MTV's award for best video of the year; the song and its popularity were part of the air of 1990.

If there is a novelty to O'Connor's reading of the song, it lies in its pointed monotony. Experience resides at an impossible distance, in another world. Nothing happens. Though not entirely lacking modulations of intensity, the vocal confines itself to a considerably narrower range of expression than any of Prince's recorded versions.[12] The video drives the point home, consisting almost entirely of a tight close-up of O'Connor's pale face against a black background as she sings with minimal expression; a black turtleneck exaggerates the effect. As befits a song tracking emotional catatonia after

love gone wrong, the affect is at once excruciating and excruciatingly flattened: an architecture of dry ice presented as a song. This arrives in shocking
counter to O'Connor's famously wide-ranging and passionate voice, as well
as to her well-earned reputation as a political scourge.[13] Beyond the nicely
detailed sentiment of the lyrics, the song *is* the tension between singer and
performance. Perhaps some of the general satisfaction was seeing O'Connor
in such a humble (or humbled) mode; this may speak at least in part to why
the song would be the only true hit single of O'Connor's lengthy career.

Therein we have a sociological reason for the song's success. But there is
another way to describe the matter, intrinsic to the song and the particularity
of its distant, echoey keen. This is in the attenuated shock of realizing that
the song is beautiful *anyway*—that beauty is possible even in this death-in-
life, this world where nothing can ever happen.

I DON'T WANT ANYBODY ELSE

O'Connor's bifurcated role as career artist and one-hit wonder—a sign of
the magnetic power of pop itself within this period—is not the era's singular case. Australian band the Divinyls, formed in 1980, managed a single
U.S. gold record in their still-ongoing multidecade span. Recorded in 1990,
"I Touch Myself" peaked at number four, a paean to female masturbation
considerably less "She-Bop" than Irigaray, specifically the famous passage
one was entirely likely to encounter in an Introduction to Women's Studies
course:

> Thus, for example, woman's autoeroticism is very different from man's.
> In order to touch himself, man needs an instrument: his hand, a woman's
> body, language.... As for woman, she touches herself in and of herself
> without any need for mediation, and before there is any way to distinguish
> activity from passivity. Woman "touches herself" all the time, and moreover
> no one can forbid her to do so, for her genitals are formed of two lips in con-
> tinuous contact. Thus, with herself, she is already two—but not divisible
> into one(s)—that caress each other.[14]

This is the figure that the Divinyls, led by singer and cowriter Christina
Amphlett, parlayed into their sole hit. There is a Žižekian delight in over-
reading the conceptual relation of this figure to the end of a divided Europe;
to the reunified Germany once again touching itself; and to the *overcoming
of a prohibition on pleasure* as freedom '90, as the logic by which pop coordinates itself with the fall of walls.[15]

Like most of the great one-hit wonders, Deee-Lite had more than one hit: the band reached the top of the Hot Dance / Club Play charts five times. And yet "Groove Is in the Heart" appears on the compilation called *The Best One Hit Wonders in the World Ever.*[16]

As is often the case, the "one hit" is the band's first; the following songs might be reckoned to have charted in part via momentum rather than their own deserving qualities. Given the number of exceptions, however, this cannot be an entirely satisfying account. An alternate (but not exclusive) explanation holds that the song is best remembered that can capture, store, and sell forward the feeling of the times; the distillation of singles down to single is in part a collusion between market and mnemonics. Cultural memory removes bad data: engaged in the operation of crafting a coherent image of an era, it is another name for ideology itself. "One-hit wonders" offer a peculiarly direct image of ideological action.

None of this is to say that "Groove Is in the Heart" is somehow a perjured song, aesthetic complicity with a beat. It is witty and original, genially mad-cap with lots going on—a soothingly surreal vacation on the dance floor. The song's ideological kernel is most intelligibly described as *postcompetitive*. Such a sensation is more unusual than it may first appear: by the time one encounters a single within the media space of mass culture, the song is already charged with competition. Having entered the arena of the Hot 100 (an abstract market space nonetheless located in the United States), the height of its climb is always at stake. This drama is intrinsic not to the song, exactly, but to the experience of the song. This is part of what is meant by the suggestion that pop is always the dominant; songs confront each other as combatants, and to become truly pop is already to have bested a host of songs both heard and unheard.

Inseparable from this is the expectation of a single's fall—often more precipitous than its ascent, in keeping with the common understanding of pop music as something that exhausts its secrets (if it has any to its name) easily and entirely. Thus the dreamy universality of the pop song is always at odds with its fate as a cultural commodity, disposable as it is consumable, destined for its paradoxical fate on classic hits radio: *oh yeah, remember when that song was timeless?*

Such a tension is part of pop's nature. The rare song that seems for a time to escape from the iron law, that endures as a hit for an improbable span, acquires a mythic sense in accord with having seemingly transcended the gravity of pop itself. The sublimity of "Groove Is in the Heart" lies in its mythic endurance, but also in the extent to which the song matched this market affect with its own, a song of such flirtatious unconcern musically and lyrically that it felt only reasonable it should elude the tensions of competition and float free—for a while—from the narrative rise and fall of the pop single.

Formed in New York in 1986, the trio was comically postnational: Super DJ Dmitri (Dmitri Brill) is from the Ukraine; Jungle DJ Towa Towa (Towa Tei) from Japan of Korean descent; and Lady Miss Kier (Kierin Kirby) from Youngstown, Ohio. This, along with their stylized, drag queen–inflected pan-sexuality, authorized a downtown utopianism: "quirky, '70s-era visual styling, combined with a positive message of peace and unity."[17] The obvious connection is to the U.K.'s rave scene; certainly the "sampladelic" house of "Groove Is in the Heart," released in summer 1990, owes much to S'Express, M/A/R/R/S, and other bits of acid house gone pop. Yet it lacks their frenetic scramble, just as it has none of Orbital's chilly logic or the KLF's ironic grandeur. Moreover, the song dallies equally with Afrocentric hip-hop, borrowing Daisy Age imagery and featuring A Tribe Called Quest's good-natured emcee Q-Tip. Reaching through this style, "Groove" gathers in funk and soul traditions as well, offering cameos from Maceo Parker and Bootsy Collins, both of whom had played with James Brown and Parliament-Funkadelic. It's a club with everyone in it; *World Clique,* the album was called.[18] "Your groove I do deeply dig," sang Miss Kier, with courtly alliteration, and then, "no walls, only the bridge."[19]

The song is finally slight, breezy, too easy to like. Anything could have stopped it; nothing did. The laws of competition seemed suspended. First it topped the Club Play charts, then 12″ Sales; it held the heights for three weeks, the charts for twenty-one, was eventually named *Billboard*'s Club Play single of 1990. It was the feel-good song of the summer, the autumn, the winter.[20] Its sheer ongoingness, its frictionless careering through the seasons, bore some genetic similarity to the time-surfeit spilling over "We Didn't Start the Fire" and "Freedom '90." The song itself was blameless, charged with a blithe omnipotence; as it persisted in the clubs into the summer of 1991, one came to suspect that we were letting it stand for something, letting it narrate a change in the world at large, one that we almost believed.

I GUESS IT'S A BRAND NEW DAY AFTER ALL

If there was something akin to a pop emergent in the period from 1988 to 1991—a dominant moving within the dominant—it was that phenomenon that began with the boy band and shortly blossomed into the broader category of teenpop.

Boy bands have always been with us, as James Miller, for example, has shown regarding the manufacture of Ricky Nelson.[21] The modern boy band, however, was born in the eighties. In 1982, Maurice Starr discovered Boston R&B quintet New Edition and released an immediately successful debut; by 1984, group and producer had parted ways for familiar fiscal reasons. Starr then formed New Kids on the Block, another group of Boston boys, though this time they were white and less distinctly based in R&B. This deracinated harmony quintet with multiple lead singers and coordinated dancing, riding a frictionless stylistic mobility within the horizons of blue-eyed R&B and rock mixed with light soul ballads, would become the formula for all future acts.

The New Kids' self-titled 1986 debut made no impact. Two years later, *Hangin' Tough* started weakly in September, and the band was on the verge of being dropped by Columbia Records when it charted with second single "You Got It (The Right Stuff)" in early 1989. The song goes about the crudely appealing business of welding hip-hop beats to the teenybopper tradition, with stiff, programmed drums initially standing out from the smooth harmonies to emphasize the novelty of the jointure, an awkward fit overcome by sheer enthusiasm.

From that point on, New Kids' success was almost incalculable—but for the fact that pop knows only calculation. A year after its release, the album hit number one; by the end of 1989, *Hangin' Tough* was the year's best-selling album. In the end it would spend 132 weeks on the charts and sell 16 million copies; the group's cumulative sales reached 70 million.[22] This makes them one of the five most successful boy bands ever: ahead of *NSYNC, Westlife, and Take That, but lagging behind Backstreet Boys' 100 million–plus sales.[23]

The female complement that would fill out teenpop is ruled by bubblegum divas (with a British exception for groups like the Spice Girls, All Saints, et al.). Lording over these are Britney Spears and Christina Aguilera, and their precursor Robyn, a Swedish teen who sold multiplatinum with the genre's proof of concept, *Robyn Is Here*. ("Swedish" is increasingly operative code: the Maurice Starr mode ceded pride of place in the nineties to more stylish Swedish producer-songwriters, most notably those associated with Cheiron Studios, Denniz Pop [Dag Volle] and his protégé Max Martin [Martin Sandberg] foremost among them.)

Per the rules of pop reception, teenpop's core appeal was equally the excuse for its thrashing. Despite the music's sophistication, it has been generally dismissed along familiar lines for its trite sentiment and anodyne appeal, as well as its formulaic nature: "After the opening, nearly grown-up song, kiddie-pop albums grow sappier fast," writes the *New York Times's* lead music critic. "They have you're-the-one songs and after-the-breakup songs and self-esteem songs and dreaming-of-you songs. Most groups also have a pious number praising God, parents or both, all in the most unctuous harmony."[24] Accurate enough in its thematic way, such an account remains entirely unable to get at the music's specific appeals, or to take seriously the desires of a considerable swath of humans. Ironically, the critical response tends to reproduce the very failure it identifies: as clichéd and universal as the clichéd repetitions it decries while insisting the genre's appeal is itself emptily universal, without historical particularity.

This critical condescension corresponded to the common feminization (and gay-baiting) visited on the boy bands and the patronizing of female singers detailed by scholar Gayle Wald, wherein a "high/low hierarchy is based around notions of the fickleness, superficiality, and aesthetic bankruptcy of the material forms that girls' desires take in popular culture." One might add that this gendering of teenpop redoubles the identification of pop and of female-identified art as outside of history, isolated in spaces domestic and diminished. Wald, interestingly, locates this as a process unfolding over the course of the nineties, "the trajectory of a decade-long decrescendo in popular music."[25]

Abject, feminized, and inauthentic: *NSYNC, Backstreet Boys, and Britney Spears (with each album magnetized by the writing of Max Martin) dominate the list of best first-week sales—an all-important industrial indicator—for all genres and years. At a distance it's not difficult to discern the constellation of reasons: the intricate melodies defined by surprising key modulations, along with the successful deracination of rhythms borrowed from the urban charts, begin to offer a persuasive explanation. One of the nineties' primal market imperatives was to sell rap to reticent portions of the U.S. and global market, but without rappers—or at least without Black rappers, of either the Black Nationalist or gangsta persuasion (accordingly, the only album to challenge teenpop's series of records for first-week sales was Eminem's *The Marshall Mathers LP*, which shifted 1.7 million units in the spring of 2000).[26] This is the thoroughgoing truth of teenpop: blue-eyed hip-hop plus the finest melodic technology yet developed, offered up for the delectation and identification of adolescents in a decade coincident with an increase in demographic power and disposable income among teens and tweens—a market that began to contract around the millennium.[27]

Teenpop's mature form, one might say, arrived with *Hangin' Tough* and completed its formation with the opening of Cheiron Studios in 1991 and its recruitment the next year of Max Martin; during the period covered by the present study, it was in the process of becoming the leading edge of the dominant. Even more striking, however, is the periodization of teenpop in full. Born around 1989, it declines sharply in 2001.[28] Teenpop is the dominant's dominant for the dot-com boom and Pax Americana—the very figure of the endlessly expanding market as celebratory stomping ground for risk-free adolescence, to revise a title by X-Ray Spex.[29]

FEELING LIKE YOU'RE SPELLBOUND

The Swedish songcraft that would migrate toward the market's imperial core, eventually coming to sound more American than American pop, has an elaborate genealogy that flows from the seventies and eventually becomes the cataract of what might be described as the Cheiron School of Pop which dominates the millennial moment. The most successful Swedish group in history, after ABBA, falls between those two points—and inevitably, has their greatest success in the United States between 1989 and 1991, when they produce two platinum discs and four number one singles in the United States alone, en route to 45 million units in combined sales.

If there is a pop single that in its form and content reaches jubilantly after life beyond care, beyond prohibition, beyond *event*—reaches after the entire congealed affect of the era—surely it is the last of these singles, which peaked in May 1991: a kind of realization of the completed moment. Farewell to an idea, or to a few; Roxette's song is in several regards a synthesis of elements already seen, a demonstration of the ways of understanding the passage coming to an end, a nightcap for the new morning. Summoning first the light psychedelia of sixties counterpop (especially "Magical Mystery Tour," from the intro's hubbub and tour guide through the video's requisite enigmatic tour bus), the song's milieu is nonetheless of its own moment—the moment of Deee-lite, the Da.I.S.Y. Age, Stone Roses' "Fools Gold." Per Gessle's melody—surely having learned as much from Lennon-McCartney as any song of the period—is in turn pure 1991.

Except more so. Within a hundred seconds the song has generated five or six separate melodic parts, each one a hook (*Don't Bore Us, Get to the*

Chorus!, as the title of one hits collection demands),[30] which it proceeds to snap together in varying configurations before arriving at an instrumental break that leads into *another* bridge and a chorus fade—all in a bit more than four minutes. The profligacy is dizzying, perhaps even exhausting, an aerobatic inventiveness insisting that anything is possible. The order of the parts doesn't matter; this is the meaning of the song's form, the endlessly reconfigurable hooks. Pleasure, mobility, infinitude. *Feels like flying.* The song is called "Joyride"—how could it be anything else?—and horizonless transit is everything. Cars, trains, planes, balloons, and no particular place to go, but everybody's going there: "Hello you fool I love you: come on join the joyride." Things get more imperative: "Be a joyrider!" Promises come easy: "I'll take you on a sky ride, feeling like you're spellbound." Yes, that's it exactly: the spell, the inexhaustible glide, "sunshine is a lady, rocks you like a baby," *whatever.* There will be no coming down; the trance that never comes up hard against anything is the very sign of freedom. "It all begins where it ends," and that's the good news, every straight line—time's arrow, space's borders—having been vanquished. This is Roxette's second most historically charged song.

THE DEATH OF VINYL

The vinyl age ended in 1989. Pressed first by audio cassettes and then by the 1982 introduction of compact discs, the LP could eventually claim neither low cost nor high fidelity, ease of use nor durability. Released in 1948 and regularized in 1952, the Long Playing record, as is well known, shares a history with rock 'n' roll and with modern pop music—a relationship that begins to explain the attachment of music fans to the format. That attachment is so mystificatory that it deserves in full the term it earned: *vinyl fetish.* It appears sometimes as a belief in the objective sonic qualities inhering within the material, sometimes as a perversely nostalgic yearning for a barely bygone moment, mistaking a marginally older form of commodity, some just-passed instant of capitalism, for an artisanal Eden. Resistance to the relentless intensifications of the market is stored in strange places.

That said, the digital format would generate substantial and unforeseen changes in the music market, following on a decade of acceleration in easy, efficient file sharing allowed by the technology and the major labels' white-knuckled aversion to confronting their own logic.[31] These changes manifested as industrial crisis just around the millennium, after Napster's appearance in 1999 and the 2001 court decision that shuttered Napster but failed utterly to put the genie of digital file sharing back in the bottle. This crisis resulted in the not-yet-resolved dual action of increasingly centralized and monopolistic wagon-circling within the recording industry, and expanding networks of quasi- or noncommercial circulation beyond it (the irony being, from the perspective of the vinyl-cherishing resister, that the new technology proved much more of a challenge to corporate regimes than did clinging to the old).

Even before that crisis, however, the digital shift resulted in restructurings of the music market. Significant among these was the rise (or return) of the single song as the fundamental unit of pop music: the random-access programmability of the compact disc meant that individual tracks could be selected, reordered, repeated (and eventually ripped as independent files). This entailed the parallel ascent of the producer's power in relation to the band, a scenario already implicit in the production methods and materials of rap and acid house, and eventually much of the teenpop mentioned herein.[32] This change at once wants its own accounting and shouldn't be exaggerated; the grouped and even coherent cluster of ten to twelve songs which the LP had canonized remains a popular format.

Still, the change is decisive. We have already seen in pop its affinity for the spirit of the times (in a way that it was not equally well suited for the cultural situation of, for example, "the sixties"). But if that traces pop's affective timeliness, the renewed emphasis on the form of the single correspondingly supplies a technological basis for a pop belle époque, given pop's own identification with the hit single, the Top 40, the Hot 100.

This latter belle époque, then, has its own history, distinct from the flowering of the pop single that peaks around the summer of 1962; a history that includes the death of vinyl. It would be specious to date this mortality too exactly; we have merely the *appearance* of a punctual moment, a semifictive tipping point when a process reveals itself suddenly as more advanced than casual observers suspected, indeed presents itself as an inarguable fact.[33] And in this case the moment can be supplied a relevant date—say, the actual date on which the first song reached number one on the Hot 100 without ever having been released as a vinyl single, indexing the end of the market's need for such an object.[34] As it happens, the chart in question was posted on November 4, 1989, and was good through November 10—which is to say that the death of vinyl and the end of German partition are exactly contemporaneous. The song in question lasted at the top for one week only. By strange chance, it weathered the peak just long enough to be the number one song in the United States when the Wall fell: that opus of vague sentiment which is "Listen to Your Heart," by Roxette.[35]

It's somehow fitting that, at this juncture of illimitable historical particularity, the most popular song at the heart of Western popular culture would have a title of such perfect indifference—not an indifference to events that it had neither the obligation nor foresight to record, but an indifference to any particularity at all. As a title and as a composition, one could scarcely imagine a song more determined to prove that there really is a genre called pop, recursively defined by its own capacity for the generic.

This is not to fault the song, which is remarkably well wrought without claiming any exceptionality–the kind of product that scales the charts regularly enough. Sung by Marie Fredriksson, the verse departs from one quavering minor and ends on another, the only time this latter chord appears; the chorus fits a somewhat more ascendant melody to almost the same progression. No one's breaking free: it's a sad song, after all. The structure then flashes a compositional maneuver of some difficulty, returning that orphan minor as a major chord to start the bridge in a different and surprising key, almost unmoored, and then finally spiraling upward to the chorus, now modulated a full third of an octave higher.

It's rather thrilling, albeit in a technical sense—the thrill of the beautiful machine. Accordingly, it knows the rules about how to match the form's affect with the right rhetoric. Stuck in the minor, you have "the feeling of belonging to your dreams"; the extraordinarily mobile key shift in the bridge remembers "when love was wilder than the wind." They are clichés, of course; Fredriksson sings them like she is revealing the mysteries. That's the lyric; the whole structure in which it falls has its own communication. *I know what to do with clichés;* this is what the song has to say. *I know how to snap the parts together and get you to feel that thrill despite yourself.* None of these devices— chorus setting a different melody using the same progression, unforeseen key change, striking modulation for the big finale—is a recent invention, though the coordination of all three will turn out to be characteristic of teenpop, specifically the Max Martin/Cheiron method. In some degree we are hearing a billion dollars of period style coming into focus.

But we are hearing the instant, too, and this matters. Even amid all the generic technique and vague sentiment, we are hearing the late fall of 1989. By now the argument is familiar: there is something historical in this song's desire for utter ahistoricality. "Listen to Your Heart" strives almost to the point of parody for the generic universality of which pop, justly or not, so often stands accused. This is neither an insult nor a secret; it was, according to its writer, simply the design. "The Big Bad Ballad," writes Gessle, describing the song. "This is us trying to recreate that overblown American FM-rock sound to the point where it almost becomes absurd. We really wanted to see how far we could take it."[36]

This cuts to the quick of pop's conundrum, and pop's condition in this passage. Pop is already a metagenre; Gessle here takes it as a fixed form and immediately devises metapop, not in the weak sense of "self-reflexive," but in the strong sense of a genre that puts pop through the transformations through which pop has already put genre music. This exaggeration of pop, this recreation of the abstracted sound of the market until it is ready to burst, *almost absurd*—this is the particular form of pop's unparticularity in this era. The desire of "Listen to Your Heart" is to be *the pop of pop,* and this is pop's urgency in the period animating the melodic and formal excesses, the excesses of compositional technique, the armies of supermodels and gospel choirs: to be too much pop. This is the heart of the belle époque: pop's attempt to know itself *as* excess, as a superfluity which exceeds every container, which is liberation and infinitude, a cataract in the face of which meaningful action is impossible; an excess whose dark double is a world without actual events, without direction, without change.

COMRADES, IT'S OVER!

And the Wall fell down, and on the following day there was a new Hot 100 and a new number one.[37] The connection between a single song and world-historical events, between "Listen to Your Heart" and the Fall of Europe, is evidently contingent and perhaps worse. Even if they are two facts of "the market," they seem to exist at such distant levels, in such far-flung spheres, that to relate them risks the trivial.

In order to think about the twentieth century, the century of mass culture, one must be willing to risk this—"to marry the beautiful and the trivial," to borrow the words of Raymond Roussel.[38] The century sets out to do this itself, as if it were an actor and not a stage. In a Prague theater on November 19, 1989, to choose just one example, the popular reform movement Civic Forum coalesces around the core of Charter 77 dissidents; by the end of December, Forum leader Václav Havel is elected by deputies president of the Czech Republic. In spring of 1990, Civic Forum achieves a sweeping victory in national elections; the soundtrack to their television advertisements is "Listen to Your Heart." In Hungary, Fidesz (the Federation of Young Democrats) does the same, and even integrates the title into their slogan:

Figure 10. Václav Havel goes pop before half a million in Prague, November 20, 1989. (Photo Lubomir Kotek/AFP/Getty Images)

Listen to you heart—Vote Fidesz! In Hungarian, it rhymes.[39] The song, the sensibility, are conjoined with the sense of an ending: per another Fidesz mantra, "Comrades, It's Over!"

Pop has some political use: nobody doubts this. The larger argument, and you will have seen it developing for some time, is that the spheres have made a fine bid to collapse into one another; that a motion ongoing for some time has reached, around 1989, some sort of completion; that history is now itself pop, and pop, history.

PART TWO

"1989"

(a shout in the street)

*This striving of the spectacle toward modernization and unification,
together with all the other tendencies toward the simplification of society,
was what in 1989 led the Russian bureaucracy suddenly, and as one
man, to convert to the current ideology of democracy—in other words,
to the dictatorial freedom of the Market, as tempered by the recognition
of the rights of Homo Spectator. No one in the West felt the need to spend
more than a single day considering the import and impact of this extraordinary media event—proof enough, were proof called for, of the progress made by the techniques of the spectacle. All that needed recording
was the fact that a sort of geological tremor had apparently taken place.
The phenomenon was duly noted, dated and deemed sufficiently well
understood; a very simple sign, "the fall of the Berlin Wall," repeated
over and over again, immediately attained the incontestability of all
the other signs of democracy.*

GUY DEBORD
"Preface to the Third Edition," *Society of the Spectacle*

CHAPTER 5

The Image-Event and the Blind Spot

THE END OF THIS STORY REQUIRES a return to the beginning, to a song and a sentence. The former is "Right Here, Right Now," by Jesus Jones; the latter is that of the Retort collective, naming how "American victory in the Cold War was rendered in retrospect magical, unanalyzable, by the mantra 'The Fall of the Wall.'"

We can seek to understand this claim in several ways, all of them worth pausing over. There is the matter of actual events, timelines, lived experience: how they vanish in the collapse into a single episode. Inextricable from this, there is the matter of the processes that led up to the Fall of the Wall—the antagonisms, the stakes, the ideas about how life might be lived. There is the matter of how these things survived in changed and fugitive forms, and remain as increasingly unthinkable elements in a historical dynamic itself increasingly difficult to draw into the open. Meanwhile, the word *mantra* means to get at that idea of language become not-language, repeated until its communication becomes utterly hollowed out. But (as Retort makes clear) this mantra is increasingly likely to be an image, a logo, a brand, insisting only on itself and leaving nothing else.

That the Cold War should seem to end in the flash of the image-event, an instance of Debord's "striving of the spectacle toward modernization and unification," is a contradictory fact; it may be better described as a realization than a rupture. Does not the Cold War itself, which invented its own

Figure 11. The image-event: East Berliners crowd atop the wall. (Photo Gerard Malie/AFP/Getty Images)

curious temporalities and self-concealing processes, bear a genetic similarity to the image-event? It was itself the leading abstraction in an era dominated by abstraction itself. For U.S. citizens, the combat largely presented itself as a series of distant fights and inchoate threats: communists under the bed, ideological struggle, nuclear clocks. Perhaps it would be a mistake to say that the elaborate constellation of the Cold War's end has been in main "forgotten." One might instead describe the reduction as a sort of grand, distributed desire for a concrete event to counter all that abstraction—a desire that found its satisfaction in the singular destruction of a concrete wall. An event that turns instantly to become an even greater abstraction, pretending to be its opposite. And thus we have our talismanic phrase: "the Fall of the Wall," as if it had happened all at once, had begun and ended in a day, in thirty seconds.

That the physical disassembly took weeks seems beside the point. That German unification was completed in November of 1990 is mere detail. That the geopolitical sea change, spread across years and continents, of which "the Fall of the Wall" stands as an absolute icon—that this process remains incomplete verges on the imponderable. Nonetheless, all of this is so. The Germans did not shoot out the clocks and declare a Year Zero.[1]

This is not all to make the finally slight point that "the Fall of the Wall" is not a fact but a wager, or that the Cold War didn't come to a sharp end in 1989. Rather, it means to signal the way in which such elaborate complexes get flattened into instants and, more significantly, into images: that a man standing on the crest of the Berlin Wall comes to compress a vast amount into the swing of his pickaxe, literally punctual. And it means to name this will of history to compress itself—discreetly, without much thought—and to escape into lone figures, into iconic and frozen images, in turn beamed instantly, insistently, and redundantly across much of the globe.

This is what is meant by the claim that "history is now itself pop, and pop, history." It is, of course, a reformulation of Jameson's claim that "Culture has become the economic, and economics has become cultural." This has not always been the case. But it is the endgame of the developmental logic implicit in the very idea of "the end of history," just as it is implicit in the idea of pop: the narrowing progress toward a single worldview, a universal form of social existence. No doubt the market throws off endless variation as well, as Žižek never tires of pointing out (though Brian Massumi has perhaps the clearest aphorism: "Produce variety and you produce a niche market").[2] These variations are nothing but the atomistic form of bourgeois solidarity, particles increasingly compelled to obey a single law. The logic of "the end of history" is the logic of mass culture itself.

WATCHING THE WORLD WAKE UP FROM HISTORY

—History, Stephen said, is a nightmare from which I am trying to awake.
From the playfield the boys raised a shout. A whirring whistle: goal.
What if that nightmare gave you a back kick?
—The ways of the Creator are not our ways, Mr Deasy said. All history moves towards one great goal, the manifestation of God.
Stephen jerked his thumb towards the window, saying:
—That is God.
Hooray! Ay! Whrrwhee!
—What? Mr Deasy asked.
—A shout in the street, Stephen answered, shrugging his shoulders.[3]

All history moves toward one great goal—it's almost too easy. Hegel, Joyce, Fukuyama, Jesus Jones: so goes culture's declension. Nonetheless, "Right Here, Right Now" knows something that wants reckoning, something in the passage from *Ulysses* that the philosophers miss. The unanalyzable quality of the image-event is exactly what "Right Here, Right Now" insists upon. Empty analysis, and empty representation and opinion—these are the sins of Chapman, Dylan, Prince, the lyric's villains. The song performs "the work of the philosopher: 'the glorification of what exists.'"[4] And so the song resists the temptation to falsify the occasion as anything other than an instant, a feeling. The song names in its title, defends in its verse, and celebrates in its chorus the absolute singularity of the image-event, its annihilation of time and space.

This is the internal logic of both the subject and the song. Even if it was written in 1990 and hit number two in 1991, the song and its video have become part of the complex called "1989," called "the Fall of the Wall." This isn't a mistake but an inevitability. "Wind of Change," released in 1990 and topping the charts in eleven countries in 1991, is equally inseparable from "the Fall of the Wall"—despite having been written about the Moscow Music Peace Festival and Klaus Meine's impressions of the rising tide of *glasnost*.[5] What specificity there is in the song is entirely Russian/Soviet: the Moskva, Gorky Park, the time-honored rock 'n' roll citation of the balalaika. The Berlin Wall does not appear; the song was written before it fell.

This is a measure of the power of the image-event to gather everything into itself, to become its own horizons. Pop, inevitably, loves this; Scorpions' "magic of the moment" is answered by Jesus Jones's "blink of an eye." The latter song articulates the matter more precisely, just as the song poses the precise question of pop's role at such a moment. "Blink of an eye" sees, clearly enough, that the issue here is one of visualization. We're *watching* the world wake up, after all. For the image-event, that condensed fragment of the diffused spectacle, insists above all on hypervisibility, on the reign of appearance as the triumph over historicity itself.

When we wake from history, we are not waking from the image, but into it.

Half of the video clip is standard fare, the "performance video" of a conventional rock band making conventional rock gestures. The keyboard player mostly triggers samples and otherwise entertains himself with a dance that's a dead ringer for that of Happy Mondays' resident slacker, Bez; the song's digital shuffle is Madchester all the way, dragged toward international pop. Behind the stage, projection screens display newsreel images from the end of the Cold War. People and events.

Intercut with the performance sequences are scenes of Mike Edwards "at home," if we're to believe he lives in a cramped bedsit strewn with clothes and newspapers. Well, pop singers must pretend to be the common man, when they are not being jet-set stars. His clothes and the lighting change, though the glare of the floor lamp—a domestic klieg—never dims. He never stops staring into an unseen television screen; its display somehow projects

Figure 12. Inside my TV eye: Jesus Jones, "Right Here, Right Now." (Video dir. Matthew Amos, EMI Records)

along our line of sight, playing across Edwards's face, the couch, the wall behind him. He is a screen. We're watching. He strums his Telecaster, drinks (presumably) tea, changes the channel over and over: the images are all the same. All news is one news.

If the song offers "right here, right now" as a jubilant realization, Edwards in the video is in no way jubilant, or even enthralled. He's trapped, enervated, neutralized. There is nothing for him but a numb consumption of images that cannot be entered into in any regard, can only have their blank stare returned. There is no overcoming. By the final chorus he has abandoned his distractions and curled in on himself, paralyzed. Cut to close-up. An ambiguous curl of lip, maybe a curdled smile? Light and dark patches flickering, the now inassimilable images still playing across his visage. He seems to have accepted things—no more looking for another channel, another show. And the song ends, not with a bang, but with that horn fanfare that introduces the chorus—now scaling down, a shout in the street, trailing away, a surprising deflation at the end of history. A shrug of the shoulders.

There is as much truth in this deflation as there is in the song's major lifts. If the song suggests jubilation in the escape of history into the image-event, a magician's assistant disappearing into the trick box, this feeling is not the singer's but the song's. This reduction of all meanings to one inarguable and blank fact—this unification is, as we have been arguing all along, the telos of pop itself. "Pop" in some degree *means* that expression which trades away the complexities and discontinuities of historical dynamics for a promise of timelessness, of unbounded but instant affective charge.

It is a matter of indifference whether this is virtue or vice. There is no Adornian position here that art's task is to preserve a space against the thinning of real experience, any more than there is a celebration of evanescent pleasure as a sufficient end in and of itself. Nor is there a disingenuous, desperate distinction between critical and complicit genres within the marketplace.[6] Pop songs are ideological hosannas, no doubt. They are phantasms of transcendence and transfers of capital. Songs are in some regard opportunistic—calculating communicative possibilities available within real contexts. They are as well sensitive traps for fleeting affects and hidden suspicions, and even for nuances and fissures within these. They can thematize a situation, intuit its shape, render up its affect. They can be used by an audience to explain something to themselves, to experience intensely something otherwise hard to articulate, to store an occasion or feeling for later.

These are summary facts, perhaps even truisms. One periodizing claim that must in some degree trump these for its specificity is this: our signal song's contradiction between exultation and deflation is *about* something, something entirely specific to the moment. We shall return to this. For now let us hazard a periodizing claim about the exultation as an independent fact.

Pop experienced such dramatic emergences around 1989, such grand flights, because its moment had arrived. In this matter "Right Here, Right Now" testifies for its cohort. It wants to register above all the unanalyzability of the completed and unified spectacle *as* the truth, as the Real of History—"that which resists symbolization absolutely."[7] "The end of history," the triumph of liberal democracy and of the market so massified it achieves immanence: this is the idea pop had been waiting for since its beginning, the set of conditions in which it could make the most sense. This is what it means to say that 1989 is the beginning of a belle époque for pop. *I was alive and I waited, waited; I was alive and I waited for this*—this is pop itself singing, making its own true confession.

But that's not quite right. It's a kind of idealism, with pop as an autono-mous actor haunting the wings until the time comes round for its aria. Why should we not think it's empire singing, using a pop song as its prosthetic throat?

This must be part of it as well. There is not, cannot be, a belle époque for pop alone. If pop, to restate the situation, had always meant to be a triumph over time, it was bound to realize itself at this moment, which had as its core meaning a triumph over time, inextricable from the collapse of historical opposition. Clocks will still run in circles, but nothing can *happen*—this is the sense that one returns to over and over after 1989, phrased a thousand different ways. This is the ambiguous exultation of America's geopolitical belle époque, the seeming restoration of its glory as global hegemon, a glory greatly tarnished over the previous quarter-century. The period from 1988 to 1991 is, for both pop music and the United States, the emergence of this new formation. It is the antechamber of the unipolar world, of the Washington Consensus and the last Pax Americana, which contains within it the spec-tacle of the nineties economic boom.

This congealing of historical process into a pseudo-concrete thing in turn allows antagonism *as an entirety* then to be subjected to "the absolute decon-struction" (the phrase that appears, inevitably, in an Absolut Vodka televi-sion spot, superimposed over iconic footage of the Berlin Wall with crowd perched atop, one man wielding a pickaxe.[8] Such cultural effluvium might cause spasms in any but the most somnolent viewers; perhaps it is meant to. Is the man with the axe somehow also Jacques Derrida? It was only in 1987, after all, that Derrida published *Of Spirit: Heidegger and the Question,* taking up the question of deconstruction's intellectual-historical relationship to, among other things, Nazism. In 1993, Derrida published *Specters of Marx,* a timely, even symptomatic, meditation on the eponymous tradition.[9] The two texts bracket 1989's "absolute deconstruction"; the ghosts of National Socialism and Marxism both crowd around the Wall, and its Fall. For all that, it is the casual and contentless name-dropping that marks the Absolut spot: the imbricated and complex intellectual tradition is instantly swallowed by the image-event, just another part of the triumph of liberal democracy. All that and more; there is enough irony nestled in the fact that the product at hand is vodka—the national liquor equally of Russia and the Soviet Union—to drive one to drink. Through this artifice, all antagonism seems to have been undone, canceled—but this is an engineered appearance. The surfeit, the excess haunting the image tells us otherwise; if we have learned anything from deconstruction, it is this.

That is the full span under the sign of uncontested U.S. power and the untrammeled expansion of markets. This boundlessness, this absence of barriers literal and figurative—surely "the Fall of the Wall" stands for this as much as for the specific unification of Germany or the pulling aside of the Iron Curtain. Surely this unbounded sensation is the same as that of the sense of the end of history: a spatial version of the temporal account, a map painted in a single color to match the triumphal, monotonous unfolding of empty time.

This is the political sensation that meets itself in music determined to elaborate the unfettered feeling, the boundlessness, along a variety of axes—starting, as we have already seen, as a kind of excess that cannot be analyzed or contained, the complement of which is an inability to experience actual events. The absence of limit and ground for experience is a kind of fairy tale that pop music had been recycling since its dawn—at least since the opening credits of *Blackboard Jungle* in 1955, scored to Bill Haley & His Comets' "Rock around the Clock."[10] Finally history had come out to meet pop as something more than a fairy tale, or something less. A truth, a way of being.

BOB DYLAN DIDN'T HAVE THIS TO SING ABOUT

Pax Americana proved no more pacific than any other Pax. It was a picture of the world, but one with the power of fact; the picture was hard to shake. The Gulf War (not yet "the First") arrived in the summer of 1990; already, it seemed part of a different reality. In the ease with which U.S. force brought the belligerents to heel, so distinct from Vietnam, the Gulf War seemed to confirm the new situation.

As a social matter, however, this conflict was not without its mnemonic character. At the Grammy Awards on February 21, 1991—while the military mop-up slouched toward conclusion—Bob Dylan received a Lifetime Achievement Award. It was bound to be an odd occasion, not least because of Dylan's well-known recalcitrance in the face of such institutions. Moreover, despite the soft-focus generalities of "Lifetime Achievement," it was a specific occasion designed for polemic. At the same time, there was a sense of Dylan as a revenant from a different historical milieu altogether (fostered in part by his ongoing turn toward music from earlier eras, previous centuries)—as being out of time.

He sang a song from 1963, "Masters of War," tamping the melody into the tempo and collapsing the words into a glossolalic yelp. In the description of Greil Marcus, "It was an instantly infamous performance, and one of the greatest of Dylan's career. He sang the song in disguise; at first, you couldn't tell what it was. He slurred the words as if their narrative was irrelevant and the performance had to communicate as a symbol or not at all."[11] An artifact of the Cold War's apparition as ascending disaster in Southeast Asia, it's a song of absolute antagonism directed at its titular villains: "I hope that you *die,* and your death will come *soon.*" Twenty-eight years later, the song was surely his most timely and his most out of time; it was hard to say if he was trying to make it mean again through the performance's distortions, or burying it for good. He followed this with a gnomic acceptance speech, as uncomfortable as it was brief.

Well, my daddy, he didn't leave me much, you know he was a very simple man, and he didn't leave me a lot but what he did tell me was this, he did say, son, he said—he said so many things, you know?—he say, you know it's possible to become so defiled in this world that your own father and mother will abandon you and if that happens, God will always believe in your ability to mend your ways. Thank you.[12]

The odd peroration (borrowed from Psalms 27:10) is as telling as the performance and Marcus's account of it, telling about what might and might not be possible at this belated moment. It is a study in not taking the bait—scarcely a new trick for the old dog. But there is something peculiarly *of the moment* within it—an adaptation to new conditions, to a changed world-picture. The song cannot suddenly lack antagonism; it is nothing else. But the Real of History, the new Real in its glory, can only be approached by symbol, by affect. It's buried deep in the performance, sublimed out of the lyrics—*as if their narrative was irrelevant*—and unmentioned in the speech. Like the unmentioned occasion of the Gulf War, and the larger occasion of the end of the Cold War, the antagonism is still somehow present: as context and feeling, as a ghost and an absence. It cannot be represented directly. This should by now be familiar.

CYNICALLY SAY THE WORLD IS THAT WAY

This loss of narrative has presented itself earlier, most evidently in songs that try and fail to make a story of the times. But of course the sense is every-where in the music this book has considered: in the triumph over time; in the *ekstasis;* in the absolute, empty domination of the present moment; in the inability to imagine what might come next, and the lack of an urgency to do so. We have scarcely had occasion to mention the best-loved song by British alternative pop act the Sundays, "Here's Where the Story Ends." The lyrics are opaque, as if the story already can't quite be recalled. "It's a little souvenir of a terrible year," choruses Harriet Wheeler, hiding nothing and everything. The song is from 1990; we never discover what the "it" is.

Narrative failure, it scarcely needs to be said—the end of story—is another way of naming the *thought* that is "the end of history." This is the very sense in which Fukuyama's proposition deserves attention as something more than mere neoconservative wish fulfillment. It is the pop flipside, the form taken within the public imagination, of Guy Debord's less catchy descriptions: "The spectacle, being the reigning social organization of a paralyzed history, of a paralyzed memory, of an abandonment of any history founded in historical time, is in effect a false consciousness of time."[13]

For Fukuyama this abandonment of any history founded in historical time is an overcoming; for Debord, what must be overcome. For both it is the situation. The question before us, finally, is not whether pop music understood this situation—by now this book's opinion on the matter is obvious. Rather, the question is whether pop music was able to have more than a triumphal sense of how things stood around 1989, as the new conjuncture was coming into view and asserting its absolute quality.

How, then, can this conjuncture be described? At one reach we have mantras and codes; at another, theoretical conceptions. Between these, there are something like facts. These include the replacement of almost all Eastern European governments with bodies above all not Communist; the disintegration first of the Eastern Bloc, and then of the Soviet Union; and then the turbid chaos of the Russian Federation, turning its shambling bulk toward the global market. In skewed parallel, the People's Republic of China refashions itself from Deng Xiaoping's "Socialism with Chinese Characteristics" into a furnace of state capitalism. This all seems of a piece with the popular wisdom, the linear narrative in which the last actors rise up against the failed promise of socialism—against themselves, if necessary—and in favor of the democracy of the market. This happens everywhere and at once.

What does the pop version get wrong? For one thing, the cycle of governmental conversion starts earlier, and it is not as unidirectional as one might suppose; South Korean protests "finally brought down the authoritarian Cold War government in the 'Great June Uprising' of 1987."[14] The deposed government in question was of course not communist but a military-corporatist state. This is a comparatively minor example of the inconsistencies that vanish in the dust of the Wall's demolition, but a suggestive one. The coherence of the global events in 1989 is in many ways a perspectival effect, a function of one's aperture. Signal in Fukuyama's vision is the need to claim at once an Archimedean stance overlooking all of history, and an aggressively framed reading of specific political changes in the latter portion of the twentieth century. The story of Chile, for example, indicates the crudity and misprision of his line of reasoning. Fukuyama declares, without inquiry, the three-stage sequence of the overthrow of Allende's socialist government by Pinochet's U.S.-orchestrated military junta, in turn displaced by a "popularly elected government" in 1988, as simply another confirmation of the last remaining narrative.[15] In so doing, he offers an elective blindness to the obvious fact that Allende was himself democratically elected, that there is no intrinsic contradiction between socialist policies and popular elections, and that the victory of the Concertación Party in 1988, as Fukuyama composed his account, took place inside a narrative of fracture within, and in turn *against,* the Southern Cone neoliberalism exported and installed by the beacon of liberal democracy, the United States.

The gross inadequacies and factual embarrassments that come from the reduction of history to a single vector cannot, as already suggested, be laid on the stoop of Fukuyama, that beautiful symptom. Nonetheless, the illusory coherence of the events of 1989 requires careful attention herein, insofar as pop both wrestled with that very illusion and even purposed to draw out the incoherence and insufficiency of the monolithic official story.

A LITTLE SOUVENIR OF A TERRIBLE YEAR

If the images of Berlin were best able to condense the experience of historical culmination into a symbolic unity for the West—if "the Fall of the Wall" became the pop moment par excellence for the Anglobal narrative—the events have no greater claim on world-historical significance than those that unfolded in the vicinity of a quite different architecture. The events in Beijing might be distinguished from those in Europe in part because, more seemingly exotic from a physical and cultural distance, they availed themselves even more of ideological misrepresentation.

The foundations of the occupation and the massacre of the occupants in Tiananmen Square have been widely and conveniently misrecognized, with help from many sides. Predictably enough, Fukuyama requires that the drama follow the same script as every other: "The revolutionaries who battled with Ceaușescu's *Securitate* in Romania, the brave Chinese students who stood up to tanks in Tiananmen Square, the Lithuanians who fought Moscow for their national independence, the Russians who defended their parliament and president, were the most free and therefore the most human of beings."[16] The leveling of these various confrontations is striking, and none more so than the inclusion of the "brave Chinese students."

Much is left unthought in this. Consider the occupation's own iconic image, surely one of the most reproduced images ever; it provides a complex but signal formula for this reduction, this unthinkability. And it does so in part by its very simplicity. A man stands before a Type 59 tank—a line of them, in fact. It is June 5, 1989; the bloody suppression has already begun. In the video footage we see him move repeatedly to block the cavalry line's progress, waving his shopping bags to do so. This last gesture has a kind of total pathos. Man vs. tank, shopping vs. totalitarianism. It is too good to be true, but it is entirely true. Shortly he clambers onto the lead tank, has a word with the driver, and is eventually absorbed back into the crowd. But in the picture we do not see the crowd or the driver; just the man in his work clothes posed against—importantly—*multiple* tanks.

It is easy enough to register this as a heroic moment of a single, fragile body against the amassed power of the state, literally faceless. This is very much the suggestion of *Time* magazine, which named the "Tank Man" as one of the "100 Most Important People of the Century" (a Hot 100 of humanism, as it were): "one lone Everyman standing up to machinery, to force, to all the massed weight of the People's Republic—the largest nation in the world, comprising more than 1 billion people—while its all powerful leaders remain, as ever, in hiding somewhere within the bowels of the Great Hall of the People."[17]

The vision of the individual resisting totalitarian power is well suited to the liberal promise that its own machinery is in fact nothing but individuals, increasingly free from the dictates of centralized power and ideology; the converse of this is that the individual asserting himself stands thereby always for liberal democracy, poised against the coercive state. Because this photograph and not another—say, of the thousands occupying the vast, open commons in the center of Beijing—comes to stand for the entirety of what happened, we are disallowed from seeing the events of Tiananmen Square, of China in 1989, as a conflict between groups. Simultaneously, we are asked to recognize this as a confrontation of one idea, liberal democracy, against another, totalitarian communism. This is the received meaning of the picture—a meaning only reinforced by its capture within the matrix of worldwide democratic revolution proved in Berlin five months later. As an image of courage, the picture is inarguable. As a map of political antagonisms, it is something else altogether.

The scholar Wang Hui, who was one of those students in the occupation, argues in persuasive detail that the protests were not prodemocratic confrontations with a repressive Communist government—and moreover, that these categories simply don't work in the Chinese context. Rather, the occupation was an attempt to pull Walter Benjamin's emergency brake on the government's headlong race down the capitalist road and into the global market.[18] "The 1989 social movement," Wang writes, "originated out of a general protest against the unequal devolution of political and economic power, out of dissatisfaction of local and Beijing-based interest groups with the central government's policies of readjustment, out of internal splits within the state, and out of the conflictual relations between the state apparatus and various social groups."[19]

The social theorist Giorgio Agamben approaches this puzzle from the opposite direction; against Wang's enumerated specifics, he focuses on the lack of particulars.

> What was most striking about the demonstrations of the Chinese May was the relative absence of determinate contents in their demands (democracy and freedom are notions too generic and broadly defined to constitute the real object of a conflict, and the only concrete demand, the rehabilitation of Hu Yao-Bang, was immediately granted). This makes the violence of the State's reaction seem even more inexplicable. It is likely, however, that the disproportion is only apparent and that the Chinese leaders acted, from their point of view, with greater lucidity than the Western observers who were exclusively concerned with advancing increasingly less plausible arguments about the opposition between democracy and communism.[20]

Whether Wang's variegated set of tendencies or Agamben's indeterminate "singularity," there is no position from which the Chinese events can be seen as a Manichaean political struggle.

Thus the surpassing strangeness of annexing the Tiananmen Square resistance to the story that climaxes with "the Fall of the Wall." However much such a consolidation is the inexorable logic of the image-event, it provides as well a sense of its vanishing internal contradictions, condensed into granules within the otherwise homogeneous texture of a unified meaning: the historic victory of capitalism over socialism.[21] And exactly because China's social movement of 1989 was suppressed with blood, this required (if illusory) meaning at the end of the story was confirmed. As Wang puts it, "The two most important events at the end of the twentieth century were the failure of Eastern European socialism and the reorientation of China toward the global market through its 'socialist reforms.' They brought to a close the Cold War conflict between two opposing ideologies."[22]

THE CONCEPT OF THE POLITICAL

This situation, and the thought that accompanies it, finds an early interpreter in the German jurist and political philosopher Carl Schmitt. Writing between the wars, from the medial caesura of the Weimar Republic, he devises the idea of *neutralization*. "What does this word mean?" inquires political historian Gopal Balakrishnan.

> Carl Schmitt understood it to be the foreclosure of an epochal contention that leaves behind a political and intellectual field, initially devoid of a primary, structuring antagonism. So conceived, it captures some of the salient contours of the world ideological scene that emerged after the late twentieth century collapse of Communism and anti-colonial nationalism. The disqualification of the very idea of revolutionary politics that has defined the moment, eventually led to a slackening of efforts of reform, as this term was once understood. Rounding out this picture, the withdrawal of these anti-systemic states and movements opened up vast, new spaces for the remorseless consolidation and expansion of capitalism, and for a brief moment, the march of liberal civilization seemed to extend indefinitely into the future.[23]

The ground for Schmitt's formulation is distant from the terrain of 1989; ample time has passed for both mutation and intensification. An adequate accounting of the situation must reckon both with his prescient figure and with our distance from his moment. Of Schmitt's acuity there can be little doubt. From the vantage of 1929, he concedes that "capitalism and communism are mutually exclusive," and further that "today Berlin is closer culturally to New York and Moscow than to Munich or Trier."[24] However, in Schmitt's accounting of neutralization, "always the newly won neutral domain has become immediately another arena of struggle" where the fundamental structure of antagonism reasserts itself.[25] The post-1989 period is characterized precisely by the seeming absence of such a plastic reassertion and the corresponding loss of bearing and narrative; such is the strongest case to be made for the truth of "the end of history." Had Fukuyama the insight to see the condition as temporary and uncertain, rather than final and triumphant, he might be better remembered as a thinker than as an apologist for the dominant regime.

This, then, is the situation. The antagonism that had been the story of the century, that provided for its structure and thus its navigation, has vanished—to be replaced by "this effacement of narrative coordinates and conceptual distinctions."[26] The experience of this vacuum, left when structuring antagonism disappears and is not reinstated, manifests itself equally as a crisis of culture. Perhaps Alain Badiou is correct that "during a whole stretch of the nineteenth century there existed the function of the poet-guide, with whom the absolute of art orientates people within time."[27] By the late twentieth, however, such a cultural vantage point has collapsed. This isn't a failure internal to culture, but an unfolding of the developmental logic of the market-state itself. This outcome is identified both from the Left of Debord and Jameson and from the Right of Schmitt, who intuited early on that within the logic of liberalism, "affairs of state become thereby social matters, and, vice versa, what had been purely social matters become affairs of state—as must necessarily occur in a democratically organized unit." These social matters include "religion, culture, education, the economy."[28]

And yet, confronted with the impossibility of representing the historical situation while within that situation's thronged core, pop music still manages to register at once the foreclosure of historical experience, and to develop forms, affects, and cultural schemas that cache within themselves the knowledge of what had been lost in that foreclosure, and how history might be again reanimated. Pop music around 1989 works through these very problems and possibilities, thinking a single dynamic from a series of perspectives.

AN EMERGENCE OF EMERGENCES

With that proposition on offer, the moment has come to align the various musics considered in Part One: first with each other, and then with the world-historical situation. For much of Part Two, we have been letting "pop" as such, the music of the Billboard Consensus, stand for all the genres under consideration. There is good cause for this—not the least of which is the music's status as a metagenre that potentially includes the others within it. Moreover, pop as such, the ever-dominant, could attune itself more avidly to the triumphalism of the era—a claim that verges on the tautological.

Nonetheless, the argument is that all the genres, subgenres, metagenres herein caught the wind of change, which was, in a classical contradiction, also the wind of the end of change. They did so in distinct ways—just as, it must be reiterated, they were expressions of local particularities as much as grand motions. Gangsta, acid house, grunge: these had differing shelf lives and decisive mutations, befitting their status as forms seemingly conjured from different quarters—social, geographical, musical. They require understanding along the temporal axis, as emergences, and also as apparitions and accounts of the then-current conjuncture.

The case of rap is the most problematic, for reasons altogether obvious. A musical and cultural formation based in deep disenfranchisement, rap is irredeemably, gloriously conflictual. Further, the grounds of conflict are racialized, both actually and to an even greater extent symbolically; further still, the historical particulars of this disenfranchisement are uniquely American. This is not to say that there is no global consciousness in rap's tradition. Rap's turn in 1989 is revealing in no small part because it is a shift *away* from the internationalism of Black Power and Black Nationalist hip-hop, with its allegiance both to a racial mythology of the "asiatic black man" and to the more immediate history of anticolonial struggles, especially in Africa (as well as a cultural connection to the Caribbean). Gangsta's nearer horizons, moreover, came—despite the occasional stop-the-violence polemics (especially around the Los Angeles gang truce and in the aftermath of the Los Angeles riots)— with an intensification of representational violence, even in comparison to the visions of the militarized SiWs.

However, one could argue that the international nature of the conjuncture appears plainly in gangsta's turn, through its very disappearance: an expression of the larger faith that international problems had somehow been solved, brought to a conclusion, and no longer required attention. Moreover, we have certainly charted a fundamental change in the conflict that rap conceives in the exact moment. Rejecting the social "sophistication" of the East Coast and antagonistic sound of the Bomb Squad, and further conditioned by the pressures of the culture war, legal pressure, and aesthetic attack, gangsta radically reconfigures hip-hop's social vision, conjuring a predatory street capitalism structured by the internalization of struggle—as we have named the turn from inter-group confrontation to intra-group conflict ghettoized as "black-on-black violence."

What comes into view with the rave and with acid house appears at first as the opposite of gangsta's turn: the emergence of unity. While its corollary values *peace* and *love* belong inescapably to the sixties—to a counterculture now reactivated quite consciously "without the politics"—"unity" is the pivotal creed that gives sense to the propositionally formless and massive communion, the ecstatic, apolitical collectivity of the rave. Hence it is the term that can successfully become the slogan and inverted battle cry of cultural emergence. As a self-definition and worldview, it is of a piece with the musical apparition of acid house: a formal unification of subgenres, under the technological sign of the sampler and the shamanic figure of the DJ—a development that is brief but takes on a mystical significance. Genre unity, general unity.

Capacious as any empty signifier, rave's unity discourse is nevertheless necessarily temporary. It proposes to have transcended hierarchical order in the decentered revel organized only by shared desires; the music plays back the overcoming of the traditional song form's point-to-point marching orders, and of the hierarchies of melody and harmony as well.[29] But if unity is thus *after order,* it is *before disorder;* unity's autonomous, amorphous agreements are always subject to collapse. The knowledge of unity's temporary quality is what must be repressed. Therein lies the power of the fantasy by which the rave and acid house imagine their unity as existing as a sort of recursive loop, a temporal orbital removed from linear time, beyond history.

Grunge lacks both the intra-group conflict of gangsta and the rave's dream of unity. It is indeed somewhat problematic to claim a coherent meaning for the genre, given the force of ambivalence within it. The source of this is not grunge's dual musicological inheritance from punk and metal (contrarily, grunge bears witness to the shared antisocial urgency of the two). The structuring ambivalence resides in the irreconcilability of punk's openly antibourgeois furies with the ineluctable draw of introspection—the emergence of interiority, which, however grotesque its revelations, is inescapably bourgeois in its submission to the power of psychological determinations and to the individual subject, in however much pain. The psychologizing turn of the genre should not be reduced entirely to "bourgeois subjectivity" but recognized as a late bid to make true the idea that "the personal is the political"—an urgency it borrows from riot grrrl and similar tendencies, but is unable to incorporate or articulate into a political position. The oddity of this is that many of grunge's early heroes are far from bourgeois in their formations; surely this underscores the problems cleaving both to neutralized politics and to immense success. Grunge's inability to develop a politics is in effect an inherited obligation left unfulfilled and, to add income to injury, richly rewarded.

In this, grunge is an incomplete emergence: unable to escape the trap it set, it was bound to destroy itself in the effort. Its signature self-loathing, thus, is no more the source of the genre's affect than it is an outcome of the irreconcilability; the further into the interior grunge travels, the more it betrays the social negations of the tradition of which it is meant to be the realization, and the more it must therefore sequester itself. The formal dynamics within the exemplary Nirvana song are merely the crudest testimony to the genre's vacillation, and it is plain enough that the desperate ambivalence—an inward turn that cannot be completed—is at once the source of grunge's force and its disastrous failure.

The metagenre of pop produces a meta-emergence: the recurrent figure of pop that is too much pop, that seeks to know itself *as* pop. It tries to overflow its boundaries only to discover that they're not there, that pop is the illimitable. But if it could not touch limits, this is equally to say that it could not touch anything but its own borderless sensations. Pop stands always accused of this, but it is peculiarly true in the passage of time from 1989 to 1991, as the beginning of the dozen years in which pop as such becomes increasingly identified with popular music in general. It cannot encounter boundary or conflict. It lacks a counterforce; nothing will stop it.

We might call this period "happy digital," when the form of the single—the natural form of pop as such—asserts its authority over the medium, even as it dematerializes the object itself. This eventually produces, in a dialectical reversal, a crisis for the single, the music industry, and pop as such, all around 2001. But as the happy digital era comes into view, actual dematerialization, which allows the single an infinitely swifter circulation (as it begins to leap the boundary of materiality itself), is met insistently by figures of dematerialization and swift circulation within the music: flying, joyrides, pure "freedom." These frictionless traversals are equally signs of a triumph over time, of which the increasingly central figure of the teen—that still unravished bride of time—serves as an ideal representative; for adults, the sensation is not without its difficulties. Time is frozen or flown away; in either case, real experience is necessarily gone with it.

THE MUSIC OF NEUTRALIZATION

The internalization of conflict, a depoliticized unity, the interiorization of social fury, the annihilation of boundaries: these are our four facts, our four horizons. Except they are as well a single fact, in which the absence of horizons looms large. In every case, the emergences can be coordinated by the striking absence of confrontation with an external group. This dynamic obtains unvaryingly across the genres whether or not they are happy or unhappy, peaceful or violent, social or solitary, trapped or liberated. The subject becomes the only subject, whether it be a racialized group subject, a unified and self-isolated counterculture, a troubled individual or an ecstatic one. The drama in which social groups with differing interests encounter each other in a struggle that produces change, that drives the story forward, has everywhere vanished.

That this loss of external confrontation is not a mere commonality but a determining force is revealed all the more clearly in the examples that bridge the first four chapters. De La Soul (and their cohort) offer an alternative to Black Power and gangsta rap; their style equally forges a bridge between Afrocentric rhetoric and the rave's unity. But it must also stand defined by what it renounces: that the Daisy Age's third way proves a turn away from the politics of confrontation locates it squarely within the central logic of 1989. Congruently, Nine Inch Nails' discovery of bad faith in the ecstatic throng of the rave turns not to some sort of politics but toward the psychologized interior of grunge: into the head like a hole we go, where furies can play themselves out without social confrontation.

Finally, U2 designs what is in the end a synthesis of disparate elements within the field of the moment. *Achtung Baby,* recorded in Berlin starting on the day of unification, could stand with any single document at the nexus of this book's accounts. The sounds borrowed from electronic dance music and from grunge's distorted clangor are tempered and recapitulated, according to the laws of the Hot 100. The ecstatic and hedonistic excess of rave's unity is revised as morally serious and thoroughly spiritualized; grunge's self-loathing returns in its weak form as U2's newfound irony, its mockery of rock star pretensions even as it performs them. How extraordinary a distance this is from where the band began, from the confrontational social politics of "Sunday Bloody Sunday" or "Bullet the Blue Sky." Against all this—or because of all this—the album has the highest honor, and the hardest to come by for a rock album from this late moment: the honor of being *of its time.* "A man will rise, a man will fall, from the sheer face of love like a fly from a wall," runs the chorus to "The Fly," delivering up that uncountried, frictionless flight of "Joyride," but now rendered ambiguous, sinister. Freud remarks that "the 'exciting' games of childhood are repeated in dreams of flying, falling, reeling and the like," though he continues that "the voluptuous feelings [are] now transformed into anxiety."[30] This voluptuary anxiety seems uncannily accurate to much of *Achtung Baby,* with its love songs set against the end of the world. "One," too, is a love song; they all are. But how can it not be, at the same time, the sentimental air of unification? It is the lullaby for a century which "declared that its law was the Two, antagonism"; the century which ends early, its borders and antagonisms dissolved.[31]

The music of this book, to say it plain, is the music of neutralization, the music of a situation "devoid of a primary, structuring antagonism." Phrasing it thus may suggest, if one had arrived late to the argument, that the music in question is part of this neutralization, a depoliticizing force that helps along an increasingly systematic domination of daily life. Such an understanding should not be dismissed out of hand.

However, to yield to such a conception tilts too easily into moralizing. It is well to reiterate that neutralization, as we have posed the matter, is not an activity but a condition, "the foreclosure of an epochal contention that leaves behind a political and intellectual field"; culture is part of this as well, a portion of the "world ideological scene." What happens within culture is a matter of thinking—and, moreover, such thought is capable of holding contradictory ideas within it.

Thus, to say that the music of this book is the music of neutralization is to say that it is complicitous with that frozen history—but also that it is a place where the experience of that situation is registered, where its unmappable contours are apprehended as sensations, where its pleasures and displeasures are explored, its possibilities and impossibilities.

THE TRIUMPH OF THE WEST, OF THE WESTERN IDEA

Pop music's grasp on the disintegration of the most durable confrontation known to the century is matched only by the extent to which it treats this as an occasion for celebration. In this regard, the music of neutralization joins the conservative ticker-tape parade on which falls history's last confetti. Pop music, one might hazard, has taken Fukuyama at his word. Not that hit singles were ever much in the business of "imagining a world that is radically better than our own, or a future that is not essentially democratic and capitalist"—that's not in their nature. Rather, pop immediately proclaims the resolute sequestering of furies public and personal, and the annealing of social fissures through simple commitment; it announces the end of the story itself. Events become *mere* events and escape thought, unable to figure anything without a historical ground. The music of "1989" is the inconceivability of a narrative next; it is the processless present of the image-event in which there can be no rise and fall of hegemons, no global rearrangement. Among mounting ironies, none is more barbed than that by which the great wave of emergences is structurally unable to think the new. This is Fukuyama pop.

Certainly it is difficult to find much festivity either in gangsta or in grunge. Still, both are perfectly insistent in giving voice to the neutralization. *On a plain, in my head, city of Compton*—the music's retreats are the paradoxical accompaniment to the first world's advances, now held to be completed. What need has one now for the SiWs? When Kurt Cobain swears he's a negative creep and trails off into a wordless wail, it's a matter of unspeakable pride. "Fuck wit Dre Day (and Everybody's Celebratin')": the parenthetical takes on deeper resonance. Gangsta's sonic generalizing of the sensation of threat from imminent to immanent is not some conclusory abolition of tension: in this persistence of some *form* of social antagonism we see the distance between the central conflict figured within hip-hop and the central geopolitical conflict. At the same time, it is a sound built for smoothness, for bobbing your head on Slauson Boulevard in a slow-rolling vehicle. It is the discovery of an even texture that fills the spaces of gangsta rap, replacing crisis with condition, a way things are. These examples provide a curious celebration to be sure, but provide one nonetheless, "the celebration of a cult without dream or mercy."[32]

It is easier to locate the celebration of neutralization in the rave; easier still in pop as such. "Global yet American": the pop single matches its affect to the expansive, uncontested space of neutralization—as a consumable pleasure, as surfeit, as dematerialization, as a liberatory overcoming of prohibitions. Pop becomes more pop, the dominant more uncontested in its domination. It matches its rise with geopolitical hegemony, inarguable and storyless, until the belles époques of each could be seen as one and the same.

One can scarcely overlook the symmetry in this association of pop and political zeniths. Fredric Jameson describes a 1973 movie that "set out to recapture, as so many films have attempted since, the henceforth mesmerizing lost reality of the Eisenhower era: and one tends to feel that for Americans at least, the 1950s remain the privileged lost object of desire—not merely the stability and prosperity of a Pax Americana, but also the first naive innocence of the countercultural impulses of early rock-and-roll and youth gangs."[33] What is most curious about this formulation is that Jameson is referring to the film *American Graffiti*, which locates its Eden of Americana squarely in the Kennedy-era summer of 1962. But sometimes mistakes are better than accuracy; 1962 is fairly enough the Very Late Fifties, and more accurately the end of the pop single's first belle époque. This timing is commonly understood as the calm before the Beatles and Dylan, both of whom—the former especially—appeared as brilliant singles artists before the album asserted itself as the form fitted to their contents and in turn began its long reign as the *meaningful* form of pop music.

American Graffiti locates its fantasy in the still moment just before pop universalizes itself. Mass culture on a national, a global scale has not quite been called into existence. The California town is so isolated it might as well be at the edge of the earth, and the radio station that plays "Runaway" and "Surfin' Safari" is an entirely local affair. The film's 1962 is thereby a perfect bookend to the suddenly barrierless world of 1989–1990. That is to say, the two heroic eras of the pop single are in effect leading up to and leading away from the Berlin Wall and the partition of Europe by the two antagonists.

If "youth culture" organizes the imagination of this earlier belle époque, the latter matches it by increasingly giving teenpop pride of place. This must be in part a fact not just of politics but of the market—an adolescent counterpart to the "dot-com boom" of the nineties, the buzz of juvescent *adventure capital* whirring around at thrilling, erotic volumes. Still, teenpop's reign is precise: 1989–2001, presiding over the death of vinyl and the dematerialized single, soundtracking neutralization for an audience enjoying its own moment beyond time. "Kiddie pop provides a harmless first crush, an easy transition to adult concerns, which will intrude soon enough in the lives of its younger fans," said Jon Pareles. "The music is an intermission between crises."[34] And so the Pax Americana encounters itself on the radio.

Rave's imbrication with the broader political scene is an ironic one, even beyond Tony Colston-Hayter's positioning of the rave's freedom as the liberty of the truly free market: Milton Friedman to a disco beat. His partner Paul Staines worked as well for Thatcherite David Hart's intelligence journal *British Briefing*: "[Staines] got to fire off AK-47s while supporting anti-communist movements in Nicaragua and Angola, and to drive around East Berlin in a limo just before the Wall came down, contacting dissident students and taking them out to lavish meals."[35]

For all that, the truth of rave's relation to the world situation lies in its cultural and musical form, acid house's coalescence out of house, techno, and garage into a generic unity that also appears as social unity—a celebration of the larger spirit of unification emanating from Europe Central. This sort of accounting surely has both its limits and its delights. For a moment, oppositions have been resolved; time stands still, forever three A.M. This is the exit from time that rave celebrates absolutely, though it is met by the chill sterility of "winter acid," a perfectly ambivalent expression of frozen history.

The unity is brief; it is tempting in turn to find in the rapid balkanization of acid house into breakaway scenes with intractable interrelations a muddled version of the Eastern Bloc's fate in the nineties. If this is a flippant allegory of form, it is appealing exactly inasmuch as flippant allegories of form are one of pop's most cherished devices (especially in figuring both order and chaos). A more nuanced version of this claim would suggest that the chaos of rhizomatic microgenres left in the wake of the Second Summer of Love speaks more clearly of the market opposition between collectivity and individual tastes. Unable to totalize the new situation or sustain its own contradictions, acid house falls to unassimilable fragments. And yet it is clear enough that, within its moment of ascendance and triumph, rave is trying to forge a cultural vision for a moment when politics is disallowed, leaving behind only groundless celebration. Dick Hebdige captures this diminution: "Rave and dance culture were the West's weak echo of what was called in Eastern Europe in the late '80s 'people power' as crowds gathered in the public squares of Leipzig, Dresden and Prague, not just to witness the dying days of Soviet Communism but to accelerate the process through the action of their collective witness."[36]

Here the rave is the cultural form without political content; this is perhaps the most optimistic way of phrasing the critical inversion through which "the Fall of the Wall" is experienced. The title of Hebdige's essay, "Un-Imagining Utopia," pinpoints the difference; if the crowds in Berlin witnessed a historic opening, the Anglophone west witnessed a historic closure.

HERE'S WHERE THE STORY ENDS

The closure has been described repeatedly herein, if only because the music cannot stop describing it, even when—or especially when—it presents it as an opening. It is a closure of space, now rendered unipolar; it is a closure of time, no longer open to change and thus emptied; it is a closure of meaning around the single idea of the victory of the West. This is "1989" as instantaneous and total: the closure of historical thought, in which all news is one news and finally no news, in the unanalyzable singularity of the image-event. This is one of the ways to understand the pop music of the period.[37]

Against Fukuyama pop we might pose Jameson pop. This mode is necessarily less celebratory, as Jameson's sense of history includes no fanfare for its accelerating collapse into a kind of pop itself. Jameson's method of reading is to a great extent a meditation on defeat. Nonetheless, it is able to unfold from that condition the possibility that within defeat, within historic closure, something remains: a knowledge in hiding, which cannot be seen directly.

It must be noted immediately that Jameson's method, proposed in *The Political Unconscious* and so often referred to as "symptomatic reading," is designed specifically for the study of narrative. It encounters certain challenges when presented with a cultural medium that is only provisionally so. Further, the music in question proclaims and participates in the end of narrative; that is one of the fundamental things it has to say. Further still, Jameson's method seeks out "the *ideologeme,* that is, the smallest intelligible unit of the essentially antagonistic discourses of social classes"—a vexed pursuit in this case.[38] The dissonant collage of the Bomb Squad is doubtless a sonic ideologeme par excellence, but this sound is exactly what has been overcome. In a telling inversion, the recurrent ideologeme of 1989 is the *absence* of essentially antagonistic discourse.

Still, such an optic (or auric) is one way to make sense of the very shifts tracked in pop music around 1989. If narrative's function is to render continuous a social existence whose truth is discontinuity, certainly the world picture presented by the music of the period does very much the same. But it retains within it a discontinuity, a public unconscious which is the *recto* of the public imagination wherein we began. What, then, is lodged in the blind spot of this music, the hole in its world picture? For it is after all a single blind spot shared by the genres, like the single eyeball shared by the Graeae.

Such a blind spot, where what is cannot be seen, has been identified with the Real of History, the *right here, right now* that defies representation. For pop music around 1989 the blind spot is also, as I have been at pains to point out, antagonism itself—specifically, of course, the antagonism between groups, the kind of core antagonism that can provide structure and narrative to a situation. It is this that the music says by not saying—by *insistently* not saying, by not saying with such intransigence that as a whole it finally comes to say nothing else. Antagonism and history are identified with each other absolutely—if they are not indeed one and the same, necessary to each other's being. This is an irreducibly dialectical thought: the understanding that each exists as a condition of the other, in fluid and developing forms. But it is this very fluidity, this development, that has seemingly exited the scene. Dialectical thought recognizes the loss of dialectic itself, which perhaps explains why the celebration is met by its opposite.

THE VANISHING DIALECTIC

To say this is to recognize the contradictions present even in pop's seeming flatness, its reduction and closure; it is to hear the mourning in its celebrations. Perhaps this exaggerates matters. Nonetheless, this contradiction surfaces, fleetingly but over and over, within the affects and forms of the music. The signal moment is that curious deflation in the last seconds of

"Right Here, Right Now," the fanfare's dying fall. It reveals the contradiction between the music and its subjects: pop exultant, the singer hollowed out and inert. *Bob Dylan didn't have this to sing about.* But, as the song makes clear to the singer's final dejection, neither does Jesus Jones. Not really. They get this one song, three minutes, a moment—by the close of which they realize that the *this* is already lost. By the time the song ends, "revolution" will have already passed them by as well. In the face of such a conception, there is nothing for it but to be a one-hit wonder. You can only say "right here, right now" so many times before something else had better come along, and this occurrence is exactly what the song has ruled out. Such is the outcome of, per Jameson, "the supersession of revolution as process by that of Revolution as a single apocalyptic moment."[39]

It is therefore the process through which antagonism produces narrative history that has slipped away into the night. That music possesses this knowledge is apparent in the certainty with which it lays out the situation. The antagonism is, after all, not magically conjured out of existence, but secreted away in the blind spot, unreachable. It's *there,* but—contrary to the hypervisibility of the image-event—it can't be made visible. And so it returns over and over as a sense of excess, of surfeit, of exaggeration: the sign of something present but not accounted for.

This has considerable descriptive value as an account of "the Fall of the Wall." As an image-event, it is invested with the entirety of the century's great confrontation, as a matter of seeming. Even this temporary verdict on the settling of the political landscape exists mainly as a matter of convention— it takes its social force from the fact that it is believed, rather than from a clear-eyed assessment of the scene. The conflation of *liberal democracy* and *free markets* disguises the misprisions of both terms, and the conflict between the political and economic dynamics actually at play. World-systems theorist Immanuel Wallerstein concedes that "the destruction of the Berlin Wall and the subsequent dissolution of the U.S.S.R. have been celebrated as the fall of the Communisms and the collapse of Marxism-Leninism as an ideological force in the modern world. This is no doubt correct." However, he continues by suggesting that "these same events marked even more the collapse of liberalism." The disordered world system left by the chaotic thaw of the Cold War became a hothouse for the imposition of "overtly reactionary policies." Writing in 1995, he asserts that "this rejection of liberal reformism is being implemented now in the United States under the label of the Contract With America, as it is being simultaneously force-fed to countries all over the world by the ministrations of the IMF."[40] This narrative of turbulence, force, and eventual counterforce does a better job of forecasting the postmillennial scenario of hegemony unraveling. But it is not the story that we liked to tell, liked to imagine we were living, the lullaby of the lull. The last hegemon rested, sated and righteous—a historical sleep relatively unvexed for a dozen years. All antagonism seems to be lost, but this is an engineered appearance. That which could not be compacted into the instant, that which survives as a process and not as a thing, must somewhere remain.

We have, then, two antagonisms. One has ended spectacularly with the Cold War: the hypervisible confrontation between liberal democracy and state communism. Another perseveres within the historical blind spot: that between social classes, which is merely wished away by "the Fall of the Wall." To say this is simply to name outright the distinction between Fukuyama and Jameson, or to point out the crucial process that has been effaced, rendered unanalyzable, in the substitution of politics for political economy. One antagonism has ended, one escaped.

And it is reasonable enough to presume that pop is attuned to both antagonisms. The former offers up history as pop, as universal culture. At the same time, pop, itself a fact of the national and global market, is inextricable from the conditions of that market—conditions it understands but cannot make visible, having no vantage point from which to do so. This we might call the "vanishing dialectic," which defines pop culture in late modernity and which meets its ideal explanation in 1989, when the market is suddenly all and nothing, no longer requiring analysis or remark.[41]

REVOLUTION IN PROGRESS

To make such claims, to find the antagonism of social classes hidden in the blind spot of culture, is inevitably to stand accused of enforcing an ideological weight on the rather narrow shoulders of the pop song. And yet it is hard to escape the traces of such an antagonism, however well hidden.

It bears rehearsing that acid house begins with the suggestions "Rave In Peace" and "Revolution In Progress"; the unity of this contradiction is finally the fantastical center of rave's unity discourse. But this contradiction has an actual material basis, so conveniently forgotten, in the class dialectic that is in fact the motor of the scene's formation: the confrontation between jet-setting Balearic fans and the local, déclassé Acid Teds (and at a national level, the competition between London and Manchester). As acid house ascends for its brief run as the leading music of Great Britain in 1989, it seems to have resolved this contradiction; it can come as no surprise that when it returns in mutated form, the contradiction reasserts itself in the two endgames of the rave as a leisure-market lifestyle and as a stylized political activism.

Grunge is marked by the dialectic from the start as well, in its simultaneous allegiance to and betrayal of punk's class politics, which it can neither reforge nor forget. Grunge's range of affects—its apologetics and self-loathing in an empty and isolated space—sings this failure at every turn. Its bitter ambivalence (and its incessant figuring of bipolarity, of the incoherent psyche) is thus a kind of residue, a second-order conjuration of the primal antagonism that provided the coordinates for the Sex Pistols, Clash, Mekons, Gang of Four, and a thousand others. To summon forth this charred tradition is also grunge's genius: nowhere is the failure of class politics, the distance between 1976 and 1989, rendered as forcefully as in grunge's impotent furies. It is, like gangsta, a way of preserving antagonism in the very moment of its cancellation.

Hip-hop extends the field of antagonism further, with its racialized confrontation. Still, the turn around 1989 is charged with class antagonism and with its concealment. Gone is Public Enemy's desire to "reach the bourgeois, and rock the boulevard"; in the internalization of "black-on-black violence," class categories suddenly become for the most part unspeakable, or reduced to the width of the boulevard alone in a competition to be the "most street." But that competition can communicate itself only in the terms of the most hyperbolic originary capitalism, a game of primitive accumulation that dominates nineties hip-hop. To understand this set of themes and images as expressions of corresponding activity in the genre's material base, wherein ever more capitalized entities are required to afford the new production costs of rap post-1990, merely clarifies the situation.

Of the Hot 100's relation to the market, enough has been said already; suffice to mention that its borderless, frictionless travels figure the universalization of the liberal democratic state well, but figure the neoliberal project even better, the flight of capital through endlessly opening markets, its long and susurrating whisper intimating adventures that we must know, at some mezzanine of consciousness, are happening without us. Feels like flying.

UNTIL THE END OF THE WORLD

None of this is to pose the music of 1989 as a form of resistance, as an anticapitalist polemic or even a critique along such lines. This would be a misrecognition of intent, and of mass culture, and of what political activity requires.

Pop music is a way of knowing something, something that was being busily subtracted from knowledge at just that time. Pop takes part in the subtraction, but can't help itself from preserving what it has removed; can't help but preserve some measure of depth and ambivalence and uncertainty within the singularity of the image-event "the Fall of the Wall."

It has no good reason for doing so. For the purposes of self-preservation, pop loves a market; something there is about a market that doesn't love a wall. The thing that pop knows—that antagonism is not annihilated but concealed, and that it will be needed for real history to be made again, or for history to be made real again—is in some regard testimony against itself. Such knowledge is, if anything, greatly to its credit.

But of course the songs know nothing. To claim that *what we couldn't think, pop thought for us*—this will always be a mystification, if a necessary one. It is people who know things, and they are always in need of places to store this knowledge, especially when it has been disallowed. And because the process of history is in every regard a public concern, and the desire for real experience a popular desire, it is in the realm of the public and the popular that one might seek such matters.

epilogue

The Berlin Wall is a piece not of music but of architecture, of a particularly purposive sort. It divides space and sight. This was ever explicit; if its first function was to prevent travel between East and West, its second was underscored when Kennedy visited in 1963 for his "Let them come to Berlin" speech. He arrived to discover that the Brandenburg Gate, looming over the Wall, had been hung with banners to block the view into the East. What was there to see, really? The empty zone between barriers, the apartment houses, perhaps a perspectival glance down the Unter den Linden toward Humboldt University, where Hegel was once employed? But the symbolic opacity: that is everything. That East and West, the communist and liberal states, cannot see each other is an inviolable law.

This is another way to see the hypervisibility of 1989. Each thinning of history from process to instant ends in something like an image-event. Here "the Fall of the Wall" is a special case even among special cases: an image-event *about* hypervisibility, the spectacle's spectacle. Unification and visibility become the same fact.

Unsurprisingly, architecture has taken up most immediately the rhetoric left behind by the Wall and by its Fall. Since 1989, Berlin has seen a wealth of construction, for a complex of reasons staged around reunification, driven by the ambitious alliance of states and economies that is the European Union.[1] This has become Berlin's way of processing its new situation. The architecture

Figure 13. Spreebogen: transparency in Berlin. (Photo René Ehrhardt, www.flickr.com/photos/rene_ehrhardt/)

takes many morphologies and programs, designed by architectural players great and small. Nonetheless, it has a unity nearly without challenge.

Almost any of the recent structures would serve to illustrate the new architectural spirit. It descends from the glass and iron buildings of the nineteenth century that Walter Benjamin listed as "dream houses of the collective": "winter gardens, panoramas, factories, wax museums, casinos, railway stations."[2] Benjamin himself grew up in Berlin in the shadow of one of the earliest of these, the Hamburger Bahnhof. These buildings were new forms for a new historical content, which could be described awkwardly as *the urban masses of the new consumer capitalism,* or more summarily as *modernity.* It is not certain if Benjamin glimpsed, along with Schmitt, that Berlin would be at the center of modernity's great political antagonism, the ending of which becomes the occasion for these new buildings. In that sense they deserve the name "postmodern" more than most artifacts bridled with that designation.

With a shifting vocabulary of light steel skeletons and glass skins, often slightly absinthe-tinted but rarely mirrored, the buildings contrive to announce more or less a single thing: *transparency.* You can see into them, see out of them, and the great illusion is that you can see *through* them, see the entirety of the city at once.

One does not miss the resonances of these structures, of course. They are the anti-Wall. Sightlines both literal and metaphysical are no longer blocked. The eye is unfettered, and, propositionally at least, the body and spirit as well; Berlin is an open city, synecdoche for the newly open borders of Europe as well. The buildings are "the Fall of the Wall" as a fixed fact, an architectural version of the joyride, the boundaryless, frictionless world.

There is at least one notable exception to this glass law, in Peter Eisenman's "Memorial to the Murdered Jews of Europe": a grid of weighty concrete stelae in varying heights, offering sightlines that slam closed abruptly with any movement.[3] It is hard not to conceive of the stone blocks as the remains of the Wall in some "deconstructed" form, laid out on a spare plaza. Perhaps it is a backlash to the city's transparency backlash, another blind spot. Certainly it understands the new architecture that surrounds it as part of a celebration it cannot join, being compelled to remember as surely as the transparent buildings are compelled to forget. History, blind spot. End of history, hypervisibility.

The memorial squats within the geometry that coordinates the New Berlin. The new Hauptbahnhof, filled not just with train platforms but also with a vertiginous multilevel shopping center with more lines of sight than seem possible, can look south to Frank Gehry's Deutsche Bank above the entirely rebuilt Potsdamer Platz, centering around Helmut Jahn's truly unpleasant but not uninteresting Sony Center—these form a shallow triangle with the megastructure of conjoined local, national, and international government buildings themselves, arranged along and across the river near the old Reichstag building and known aggregately as the Spreebogen.

Train station, bank/mall, and state offices triangulate the matter well. The first stands as a reversal of the famously shuttered metro and train system, the ghost stations and dead-end lines. The New Berlin and the New Europe mean freedom of movement, and just the same the mobility of capital, whirring through its open markets. These are clear enough. By the river, the state itself is now symbolically transparent as well—the secrecy, the opacity, of the Cold War having been vanquished.

Such an account surely needs to be complicated, to be scuffed up. These structures are not just *about* transparency; rather, they are a series of experiments about the sensations and ideas possible within the matrix of transparency, the regime of the hypervisible. Like pop music—and surely this is pop architecture, in the truest sense—the structures are thinking. The city is thinking. It even seems to have a brain, floating atop the Reichstag.

Largely disused since the infamous Reichstag Fire of 1933, the building was voted to be the new home of the German Parliament. Extensive repair would be required. In 1995 it was wrapped in polypropylene by Christo and Jeanne-Claude, a charivari of transparency before the reconstruction work began.

Figure 14. The visible state: rebuilt Reichstag and the allegories of architecture. (Photo Sean Gallup/Getty Images)

The stolid bulk of stone couldn't remain, of course. The building was gutted, and inside the preserved columnar exoskeleton absinthed glass plates became the new walls. At the building's head, Norman Foster's dome: a glass and steel cupola through which one can see the chamber of the Bundestag. It is the skull of the Visible State, through which the German government can be seen thinking. This is transparency taken to its rhetorical, ideological extreme.

And yet the visibility itself is ideological, fantastical. It promises that unification and transparency are the same fact, and one can feel the city soliciting agreement, trying to render such an idea inarguable. But unification, as we have seen, demands not transparency but blindness. The blind spot that music holds open—and not just music—is a kind of doubt about unification, preserved within the indubitable. If the end of the Cold War was indeed the final victory of the West, it was not the victory of transparency over opacity, but the submission of socialized space to privatized space, capital space, spectacle space, with its own blind spot, with its own time and antagonism and history still to be unfolded.

acknowledgments

I'm grateful to Laura Cerruti and Mary Francis for their trust and commitment to the prospective text; to Mary for shepherding it through and offering insights along the way; and to Rose Vekony for getting it done. Colin Dingler and Barbara Zimbalist helped in different ways with manuscript preparation, as did Kalicia Pivirotto. Seeta Chaganti was an enabling condition and deeply thoughtful as well about structural issues. The Music and Arts floor of the Berkeley Public Library was a home away from home.

This book is in many regards the punctuation to a passage that began with a photocopied zine called *jane dark's sugarhigh!* Thanks to Greta Kaplan, who let me cut and paste in her cottage and offered much other support. I owe a special debt to Evelyn McDonnell at the *Village Voice,* who hired the eponymous Jane on the basis of that first issue. Thanks also to the editors and colleagues who supported my sojourn as a music critic and helped keep *sugarhigh!* alive in various forms: Eric Weisbard, Craig Marks, Bob Christgau, Jon Dolan, Ann Powers, Will Hermes, Simon Reynolds, and Chuck Eddy. Eric also made generous space for an early and primitive accounting of the book at the Experience Music Project.

I am indebted to the many friends who've talked music with me for years. Louis-Georges Schwartz has provided endlessly suggestive responses over the duration, including the particular period in question, when he was my housemate and coined the phrase "the enigmatic tour bus." Stephen Smith, Sasha Frere-Jones, and Dan Thomas-Glass have all kept up the conversation in various ways. Chris

Nealon, who directed me to the rhetoric of Berlin's new architecture when we visited, has been equally generous with other insights and advice. These friends have been the stones against which I've been compelled to sharpen my ideas.

Greil Marcus spent ten years teaching me how to write about music before we ever met, and perseveres in that task. The book was written always with a thought for the patrons of the now-defunct 6:20 Club in Iowa City, where I worked Thursdays and Saturdays during much of the period covered herein, sometimes under the name Squarehead DJ Ivan Boesky.

This book is dedicated to Carol Clover, who is exemplary as both a music lover and a scholar.

notes

PROLOGUE

1. Katia Malausséna, "Commemoration as Staging Citizenship: The Example of the Bicentennial of the French Revolution" (paper presented at Université Paris 13/Maison française d'Oxford, April 2000), 5–9; available at www.univ-paris13.fr/CRIDAF/TEXTES/KMlpl.rtf.

2. François Mitterrand, "Press Conference on the Conclusion of the Fifteenth Summit of Industrialized Countries," July 16, 1989, www.g7.utoronto.ca/summit/1989paris/press_english.html (G8 Research Group at the University of Toronto; accessed June 28, 2008).

3. The setting, in which the song is sung to drown out German soldiers singing "Die Wacht am Rhein," is borrowed from Jean Renoir's *Grand Illusion,* made five years earlier in 1937.

4. Quoted in Paul Virilio, *Speed and Politics* (Los Angeles: Semiotext(e), 2006), 46.

5. Francis Fukuyama, *The End of History and the Last Man* (New York: Free Press, 1992), 25.

6. Translation mine.

INTRODUCTION: The Long 1989

1. Francis Fukuyama, "The End of History?" *National Interest* 16 (1989): 3–18.

2. Passing insistently through Hegel's conservative twentieth-century interpreter Alexandre Kojeve.

3. Fukuyama, *End of History and the Last Man,* 46. For all its flat facticity, the two-century unfolding is a strange story for Fukuyama to tell, as an exegete of Neo-conservative doctrine. Commentators of such affiliations as his rarely hold up the French Revolution as the birth of liberal democracy, a beacon for the future; they are more likely to proffer it as a warning against bloody Jacobin excesses, an example of history gone off the rails, and an argument against revolution as such. The tradition comes down not from Hegel's world-spirit but the corruscating irony of Edmund Burke: "Amidst assassination, massacre, and confiscation, perpetrated or meditated, they are forming plans for the good order of future society." In the winter 1997/98 issue of the *National Interest,* p. 67, John R. Bolton (later to be U.S. representative to the United Nations) draws this more familiar conservative line: "The problem many foreign policy analysts have today is that our 'French Revolution' problem is over. Our anti-communism, so passionate and so blessed by a confluence of values and interests as was Burke's opposition to France in revolution, has prevailed." That the revolution of 1789—*aristocrats to the lamp-posts!*—should equally serve as a happy first chapter for the last story ever must provoke at least a raised eyebrow.

4. This is gestured toward in Hua Hsu, "Three Songs from the End of History," *Believer* 3, no. 5 (2005): 12. The present study is indebted to Hsu's article, which takes up similar matters in brief, noting the historical positioning of "We Didn't Start the Fire," "Wind of Change," and "Right Here, Right Now," albeit without offering any particular periodizing claim.

5. United World Chart: The Official Global Hitlist, www.mediatraffic.de/alltime-album-chart.htm (viewed September 1, 2008).

6. Among the various histories of the Washington Consensus, the most piercing is that of Naomi Klein, *The Shock Doctrine: The Rise of Disaster Capitalism* (New York: Henry Holt, 2007).

7. Fukuyama, *End of History and the Last Man,* 39.

8. Raymond Williams, *Marxism and Literature* (London: Oxford University Press, 1977).

9. The place of Plastic People of the Universe in Czech social history occupies much of Tom Stoppard's play *Rock 'n' Roll* (New York: Grove Press, 2007); as will become clear later in this volume, it is of some import that the Plastics' counter-cultural squall found no purchase in the new circumstances *after* the Velvet Revolution.

10. This presupposition of cultural studies is equally its Marxian core, devolving from footnote 4 in chapter 15 of Karl Marx, *Capital,* vol. 1 (New York: Penguin Classics, 1992), 493–94. It continues, "It is, in reality, much easier to discover by analysis the earthly core of the misty creations of religion, than, conversely, it is, to develop from the actual relations of life the corresponding celestialised forms of those relations."

11. Theodor Adorno, "On Popular Music," in *Cultural Theory and Popular Culture,* ed. John Storey (Athens: University of Georgia, 1998), 197–98.

12. Here of course the touchstone is Walter Benjamin, most notably in *The Arcades Project,* trans. Howard Eiland and Kevin McLaughlin (Cambridge, Mass.: Harvard University Press, Belknap Press, 1999).

13. Fredric Jameson, "Postmodernism, or The Cultural Logic of Late Capitalism," in *The Jameson Reader,* ed. Michael Hardt and Kathi Weeks (New York: Blackwell, 2000), 227.

14. Fredric Jameson, "What's Left of Theory" (keynote talk presented at "End of Theory" conference sponsored by the journal *Critical Inquiry,* University of Chicago, March 7, 2002).

15. Jameson, "Postmodernism," 188.

16. By one measure, they had existed as early as 1965. The 1973 lineup, however, was entirely new except for Rudolf Schenker, who brought the name with him.

17. Fukuyama, *End of History and the Last Man,* 13.

18. Andrew Goodwin, *Dancing in the Distraction Factory* (Minneapolis: University of Minnesota Press, 1992), 135–36.

19. Fredric Jameson, *The Political Unconscious* (Ithaca: Cornell University Press, 1981).

20. The concrete joke had to be made once; better to get it over with early.

21. *Straight Outta Compton's* official release came in January 1989, though it had been available for several months already. See Jeff Chang, *Can't Stop Won't Stop: A History of the Hip-Hop Generation* (New York: St. Martin's Press, 2005), 320.

22. There is an argument to be had here about the relation of reggae to Bob Marley—but that genre's survival suggests that it retains some durable vitality independent of its messianic martyr.

23. The great study of pop music's fondness for the term *revolution* remains to be written.

24. Jameson, "Postmodernism," 192.

25. Retort, *Afflicted Powers: Capital and Spectacle in a New Age of War* (London: Verso, 2005), 24.

1. THE BOURGEOIS AND THE BOULEVARD

1. This book has little interest in parsing the hard-fought distinction between "rap" and "hip-hop." Generally, it is rendered as a distinction between an activity and a culture, the latter including emceeing, DJing, breaking and graffiti-writing. "Rap is something you do; hip-hop is something you live," in the formulation of the genre's early philosopher-king, KRS-1. For a more nuanced account of the terminological development, see for example Chang, *Can't Stop Won't Stop.*

2. "Public Enemy Ousts Member Over Remarks," *Billboard,* July 1, 1989, 1.

3. Quoted in Jon Pareles, "Public Enemy Rap Group Reorganizes after Anti-Semitic Comments," *New York Times,* August 11, 1989, Arts and Leisure section.

4. Quoted in Chang, *Can't Stop Won't Stop,* 87.

5. Naeem Mohaiemem, "Fear of a Muslim Planet: Hip-Hop's Hidden History," in *Sound Unbound,* ed. Paul Miller (Cambridge: MIT Press, 2008), 313.

6. Ibid., 319.

7. For an extensive listing, see ibid., 331–33.

8. Quoted in Chang, *Can't Stop Won't Stop,* 289.

9. Robert Christgau, "Jesus, Jews, and the Jackass Theory," *Village Voice,* January 16, 1990, 86.

10. The reference is to the Run-DMC lyric "Better of the best best believe he's the baddest, perfect timing when I'm climbing I'm a rhyming apparatus"; "Peter Piper," from *Raising Hell* (Profile, 1986).

11. "Don't Believe the Hype," *It Takes a Nation of Millions to Hold Us Back* (Def Jam, 1988).

12. Quoted in Robert Christgau, "The Shit Storm," *LA Weekly,* 1989, available at www.robertchristgau.com/xg/music/pe-law.php.

13. Tricia Rose, *Black Noise: Rap Music and Rap Culture in Contemporary America* (Hanover, N.H.: Wesleyan University Press, 1994), 39.

14. Theodor Adorno, *Aesthetic Theory* (Minneapolis: University of Minnesota Press, 1997), 7.

15. Dan Thomas-Glass, "The Dialectic of the Collective: Language Poetry Rap Music" (Ph.D. diss, University of California, Davis, 2009).

16. Quoted in Kembrew McLeod, "How Copyright Law Changed Hip-Hop: An Interview with Public Enemy's Chuck D and Hank Shocklee," *Stay Free!* no. 20 (2002): 22.

17. Quoted in Chang, *Can't Stop Won't Stop,* 289.

18. The most celebrated lines are

> Crucifixion ain't no fiction
> So-called chosen frozen
> Apology made to who ever pleases
> Still they got me like Jesus.

19. These three struggles together form a populist front that is in aggregate rightly understood as a "culture war"; in the present discussion, I keep to the tradition of using that term to designate a specific arena within the larger combat.

20. Mathieu Deflem, "Rap, Rock, and Censorship: Popular Culture and the Technologies of Justice" (paper presented at the annual meeting of the Law and Society Association, Chicago, May 27–30, 1993).

21. *Grand Upright Music, Ltd. v. Warner Bros. Records, Inc.,* 780 F. Supp. 182 (S.D.N.Y. 1991). De La Soul settled a similar suit, first begun in 1989, for $1.7 million; see Siva Vaidhyanathan, *Copyrights and Copywrongs: The Rise of Intellectual Property and How It Threatens Creativity* (New York: New York University Press, 2001), 141.

22. Well summarized in Deflem, "Rap, Rock, and Censorship."

23. In McLeod, "How Copyright Law Changed Hip-Hop," 23.

24. *Straight Outta Compton* is not the first gangsta rap album. Chang, *Can't Stop Won't Stop,* 210, identifies Toddy Tee's 1985 "Batterram" and Schooly D's 1986 "P.S.K. What Does It Mean?" as gangsta in chrysalis form, followed by the more substantial vision of Ice-T. As ever, what matters for the present study is that *Straight Outta Compton*—with an emphasis on the *Outta*—delivered the subcultural form into the broader cultural sphere. As to the question of whether this eventuality stems from the album's brilliance or the social situation into which it enters, the only answer possible is, "Dialectics!"

25. David Wilson, "Constructing a 'Black-on-Black' Violence: The Conservative Discourse," in *ACME: An International E-Journal for Critical Geographies* 1, no. 1 (2002): 37.

26. See, for example, Patricia Hill Collins, "It's All in the Family: Intersections of Gender, Race, and Nation," in *Decentering the Center: Philosophy for a Multicultural, Postcolonial, and Feminist World,* ed. Uma Narayan and Sandra Harding (Bloomington: Indiana University Press, 2000), 156–76; and David Wilson, *Inventing Black-on-Black Violence: Discourse, Space, and Representation* (Syracuse: Syracuse University Press, 2005).

27. Wilson, "Constructing a 'Black-on-Black' Violence," 41.

28. Ibid., 42.

29. Mike Davis, *City of Quartz* (London: Verso, 1990), 270.

30. The formalization of hip-hop's conjoining of Los Angeles and black-on-black violence can be found in a later song by Dr. Dre confrere Xzibit (Alvin Nathaniel Joiner), 2004's "Hey Now (Mean Muggin)": "L.A. on my baseball hat, where they run up right up on you with that black-on-black."

31. Chang, *Can't Stop Won't Stop,* 304–6.

32. Rose, *Black Noise,* 21.

33. This split is already clear in the foundational text of Sugarhill Gang's "Rapper's Delight" (Sugar Hill, 1979), shifting awkwardly between quotidian accounts of dinner down the block and the high life of Big Bank Hank.

34. The album of that title (Interscope, 2003), by neo-gangsta 50 Cent, was the best-selling album of 2003.

35. The voice is actually that of comedian Lady Reed, whose monologues often rhymed and were accompanied by music.

36. Chang, *Can't Stop Won't Stop,* 319.

37. *Pace* Fredric Jameson's "uneven development of modernity," *A Singular Modernity* (London: Verso, 2002), 17–95.

38. There is a larger argument to be made here about the moments that play host to such sudden and remarkable solutions to aesthetic problems. In large part because Cherry departed the pop stage as swiftly as she appeared, it was left to, for example, Missy Elliott to consolidate the rap/soul synthesis, which she did with considerable brilliance. But by then (in the latter nineties), hip-hop had won the

day; there was little sense of an opening of the field. In that regard, Cherry had no real equivalent until the arrival of M.I.A. (Maya Arulpragasam) around 2005—very much at the moment the magic spell of 1989 and its temporary renaissance of U.S. global dominion was losing its power. But we are getting ahead of the story.

39. Danny Leigh, "Chillin' with Cube," *Guardian,* February 25, 2000, Friday Reviews section.

40. William L. Van Deburg, *Hoodlums: Black Villains and Social Bandits in American Life* (Chicago: University of Chicago Press, 2004), 212; Chang, *Can't Stop Won't Stop,* 452.

41. Mike Davis interviewed by CovertAction Information Bulletin, reprinted as "Uprising and Repression in L.A.," in *Reading Rodney King/Reading Urban Uprising,* ed. Robert Gooding-Williams (New York: Routledge, 1993), 142–43.

42. Chang, *Can't Stop Won't Stop,* 374.

43. Quoted in "Poli-tricks and Pimpin,'" interview with Sam LaHoz, *Ugly Planet,* no. 3 (2007): 40.

44. The deployment of Korean-Americans as surrogate victims of predatory Black violence, and the demand for a united cultural counteroffensive, finds its most forthright articulation in presidential candidate/pundit Pat Buchanan's speech to the Republican National Convention on August 17, 1992, the closing of which is reproduced here in full (from www.buchanan.org/pa-92–0817-rnc .html):

> And there were the brave people of Koreatown who took the worst of the LA riots, but still live the family values we treasure, and who still believe deeply in the American dream.
>
> Friends, in those wonderful 25 weeks, the saddest days were the days of the bloody riot in LA, the worst in our history. But even out of that awful tragedy can come a message of hope.
>
> Hours after the violence ended I visited the Army compound in south LA, where an officer of the 18th Cavalry, that had come to rescue the city, introduced me to two of his troopers. They could not have been 20 years old. He told them to recount their story.
>
> They had come into LA late on the 2nd day, and they walked up a dark street, where the mob had looted and burned every building but one, a convalescent home for the aged. The mob was heading in, to ransack and loot the apartments of the terrified old men and women. When the troopers arrived, M-16s at the ready, the mob threatened and cursed, but the mob retreated. It had met the one thing that could stop it: force, rooted in justice, backed by courage.
>
> Greater love than this hath no man than that he lay down his life for his friend. Here were 19-year-old boys ready to lay down their lives to stop a mob from molesting old people they did not even know. And as they took back the streets of LA, block by block, so we must take back our cities, and take back our culture, and take back our country.
>
> God bless you, and God bless America.

45. Chang, *Can't Stop Won't Stop*, 420.

46. Parliament-Funkadelic bassist Bootsy Collins becomes a historical connection between East and West Coast hip-hop, having before P-Funk played bass on some of the James Brown tracks heavily sampled by East Coast rap songs in the eighties. See also discussion of "Groove Is in the Heart," chapter 4.

47. In McLeod, "How Copyright Law Changed Hip-Hop," 24.

48. Inevitable comeback attempts gain little traction; he had never really been there.

49. In this construction, beginning with his business suit and scarf on the cover of debut *Reasonable Doubt* (Roc-A-Fella, 1996), he prefigures the first season of *The Wire* (2002) by some six years.

BRIDGE: da inner sound, y'all

1. The poll in question is the "Pazz 'n' Jop Critics Poll," organized by the *Village Voice;* the 1989 results were published in a separate section on February 27, 1990.

2. Rose, *Black Noise,* 4.

3. Capsule review by Robert Christgau, *Playboy,* February 1989, 16.

4. There is actually no meaningful comparison to De La Soul's success until the breakthrough of Outkast at the turn of the millennium.

5. "De La Speaks," video interview, www.youtube.com/watch?v=Qx8tAD84 2Oo (viewed August 16, 2008).

2. THE SECOND SUMMER OF LOVE

1. Cook's sampled phrase is actually "voodoo rage"; Gerald's synthesizer memory bank famously lacked the storage to hold the last phoneme.

2. Simon Reynolds, *Generation Ecstasy: Into the World of Techno and Rave Culture* (Boston: Little, Brown, 1998), 76–77.

3. Ibid., 6.

4. "Anthony H. Wilson: Excerpts from the Interview with Eyewitness in Manchester 30 April," *Eyewitness,* April 30, 1998.

5. "Leader of the F.A.C. interview with Tony Wilson," *New Music Express,* May 31, 1986, available at www.cerysmaticfactory.info/leader_of_the_fac_nme_310586.html.

6. The relationship between the S.I. and music, especially British punk, is chronicled in one of the most remarkable cultural histories available, Greil Marcus, *Lipstick Traces* (Cambridge, Mass.: Harvard University Press, 1990).

7. Quoted in Luke Bainbridge, "A Second Summer of Love," *Observer,* April 20, 2008, 46.

8. Reynolds, *Generation Ecstasy,* 98.

9. This and only this explains the presence in the band of Bez, the very picture of Mancunian dissipation, who played maracas only incidentally while showing that the band was in the business of embodying a musical spirit, not performing a musical style.

10. Reynolds, *Generation Ecstasy*, 61.

11. Bainbridge, "Second Summer of Love," 46.

12. Sheryl Garratt, *Adventures in Wonderland* (London: Headline Books, 1998), 111.

13. Reynolds, *Generation Ecstasy*, 65.

14. The books tracing the contours of this topic are more and less rigorous. In addition to Reynolds, *Generation Ecstasy*, see for example Matthew Collin and John Godfrey, *Altered State, Updated Edition: The Story of Ecstasy Culture and Acid House* (London: Serpent's Tail, 1998); Nicholas Saunders and Rick Doblin, *Ecstasy: Dance, Trance, and Transformation* (Philadelphia: Quick American Publishing Company, 1996); and Jimi Fritz, *Rave Culture: An Insider's Overview* (Escada, Ore.: Smallfry Publishing, 1999).

15. Kellie Sherlock and Mark Conner, "Patterns of Ecstasy Use amongst Club-Goers on the UK 'Dance Scene,'" *International Journal of Drug Policy* 10, no. 2 (April 1, 1999): 117–29.

16. Peter Shapiro, ed., *Modulations: A History of Electronic Music—Throbbing Words on Sound* (New York: Caipirinha, 2000), 160.

17. The arrival of the "smiley" as logo for E and acid house dates to 1987 and the appropriation of an image from Alan Moore's graphic novel *Watchmen*. A smiley face with a blood spatter adorns the sleeve for the sample collage "Beat Dis" from Bomb the Bass, also known as erstwhile DJ and producer Tim Simenon—who would shortly collaborate with Neneh Cherry and the Wild Bunch on "Buffalo Stance."

18. D. E. Nichols, "Differences between the Mechanism of Action of MDMA, MBDB, and the Classic Hallucinogens. Identification of a New Therapeutic Class: Entactogens," *Journal of Psychoactive Drugs* 18, no. 4 (October–November 1986): 305–13.

19. Reynolds, *Generation Ecstasy*, 102. I would make the crucial, though seemingly minor, distinction of insisting that punk is defined not by "negativism" but negation.

20. Michel Kokoreff and Patrick Mignon, *La production d'un problème social: drogues et conduites d'excès. La France et l'Angleterre face aux usagers d'ecstasy et de cannabis* (Paris: DGLDT/Ministère de l'Enseignement Supérieur et de la Recherche, 1994), 273.

21. Reynolds, *Generation Ecstasy*, 81, 95.

22. Quoted in Stephen Duncombe, ed., *A Cultural Resistance Reader* (London: Verso, 2002), 120.

23. Saint-John Perse, *Anabasis,* trans. T. S. Eliot (New York: Harcourt, Brace, 1949), 60.

24. It is inevitable that these two figures, Berlin Wall and great ring road, would at some point have shared the stage of a song. And they did, in an episode obscure and mysterious enough to compel its own story, which can only be summarized here. The great American ring road anthem is "Roadrunner," the only song donated to the rock canon by Jonathan Richman and the Modern Lovers. First recorded in 1972 (an early apparition of the 1973 turn discussed above), it follows Route 128 around Boston's periphery, guitars a-jangle, impossibly attuned to mythical teen Americana. Less known is the rough draft of the song, "Ride on Down the Highway," which seems to date from near the band's 1970 formation. In a live recording from 1972 (found, misdated, on the Rounder release *Precise Modern Lovers Order* from 1991), the song is faster than "Roadrunner," and more complex—which isn't saying a lot. It has a teen couple and a fifties turn in the chorus, which the two-chord, one-teenager "Roadrunner" ascetically refuses. The latter version is everything, and nothing; "Ride on Down the Highway" is just a song. But some of the words are the same, more or less: "late at night ride down past 128 and dark outside," for example, and the swiftly sketched "Massachusetts moonlight." The song discovers for a moment the romantic vortex of the suburban landscape in which "Roadrunner" will endlessly circle, and at exactly this moment the lyric leaps beyond the vortex inexplicably, breaking the spell: "well there's a stone wall in Western Europe and I cry in the afternoon sometimes." This sudden appearance of what must be the Berlin Wall goes unglossed. It is just something like an opposite case. Immediately, as if understanding that he has lost track of a secret, he reverses direction, mumbles something about having a Coke, and goes back to talking about his girlfriend. But it is too late, and he will have to remake the song entirely.

25. Quoted in Steve Redhead, ed., *Rave Off: Politics and Deviance in Contemporary Youth Culture* (Brookfield, Vt.: Avebury, 1993), 47.

26. Criminal Justice and Public Order Act 1994 (c. 33), www.statutelaw.gov .uk/content.aspx?activeTextDocId=2156203 (viewed July 16, 2008).

27. Garratt, *Adventures in Wonderland,* 176.

28. Fantazia Rave Archive, www.fantazia.org.uk/Scene/orgs/biology.htm (viewed July 17, 2008).

29. The memorable phrase from Pet Shop Boys' "Left to My Own Devices," *Introspective* (EMI, 1988), seems to get with their inimitable refinement at the strange confluence of lushly aesthetic dance music and revolutionary chic: "In the back of my head I heard distant feet: Che Guevara and Debussy to a disco beat."

30. Unless otherwise stated, all U.K. chart data in this chapter are taken from *Billboard* magazine's weekly "Hits of the World" chart from the period 1988–2000 (vols. 100–102). That chart is in turn taken from the British trade magazine *Music Week.*

31. Jon Savage, "Machine Soul: A History of Techno," *Village Voice,* summer 1993, "Rock 'n' Roll Quarterly" insert.

32. Jimmy Cauty and Bill Drummond, *The Manual (How to Have a Number One the Easy Way)* (U.K.: KLF Publishing, 1988).

33. http://blogs.guardian.co.uk/observermusic/2008/04/we_call_it_aciiiiiiee eed_contd.html (viewed July 21, 2008).

34. *Billboard,* July 23, 1988, supplement.

35. *Billboard,* October 8, 1988, 64.

36. The quasi-acid tracks of late 1988 included D.Mob's "We Call It Acieed"; Jolly Roger's "Acid Man"; The Beatmasters' "Burn It Up"; and Hothouse's "Jack to the Sound of the Underground."

37. The sensation of the "energy flash" would become metonymy for acid house's structure, from the Joey Beltram track to the U.K. record label to the original title of Reynolds's book, *Energy Flash: A Journey through Rave Music and Dance Culture* (London: Picador, 1998).

38. "Life in a Northern Town," the Dream Academy's 1985 tribute to Nick Drake and their only hit, has little to say about the changes that occupy this book. And yet its industrial nostalgia—including a video partly filmed in Manchester— is directed unerringly at the intersection of pop and politics accompanying the end of the modern pop single's first belle époque . . . and the beginning of European partition:

> He said "In Winter 1963,
> It felt like the world would freeze,
> With John F. Kennedy
> and the Beatles."

The complementary relationship of this moment to 1989 is taken up in the book's second half.

39. Reynolds, *Generation Ecstasy,* 8–9.

40. Gimpo, dir., "Watch the K Foundation Burn a Million Quid" (The K Foundation, 1995).

41. Quoted in Kodwo Eshun, *More Brilliant Than the Sun: Adventures in Sonic Fiction* (London: Quartet, 1998), 76.

BRIDGE: I Was Up Above It

1. As one credit to the disc's materials reads, "nine inch nails is trent reznor."

3. NEGATIVE CREEP

1. Charles R. Cross, *Heavier Than Heaven* (New York: Hyperion, 2001), 154.

2. This schema of genre development is borrowed from the Hollywood cinema

study by Rick Altman, *The American Film Musical* (Bloomington: Indiana University Press, 1987).

3. Clark Humphrey, *Loser: The Real Seattle Music Story* (New York: Harry N. Abrams, 1999), 63.

4. Janet Maslin, "Successful in Seattle: Turning Grunge to Gold," *New York Times,* November 8, 1996, Movies section.

5. *New Music Express,* November 2002.

6. Liner notes to *Mudhoney: March to Fuzz* (SubPop 2000).

7. Ibid.

8. Reproduced in Jon Savage, *England's Dreaming* (London: Faber & Faber, 1991), 280.

9. Ibid., 516. Among many insightful accounts of Rock against Racism, one interesting discussion is found in Franklin Bruno's book on Elvis Costello's album *Armed Forces* (New York: Continuum, 2007).

10. Most notably in Marcus, *Lipstick Traces.*

11. The "suss laws," derived from the Vagrancy Act of 1824, allowed British police to stop and search civilians at will.

12. Greil Marcus, *In the Fascist Bathroom: Punk in Pop Music, 1977–1992* (Cambridge, Mass.: Harvard University Press, 1999), 4.

13. Savage, *England's Dreaming,* 197.

14. "David Markey's 1991 Tour Diary," www.wegotpowerfilms.com/archives/91_tour_diary.html (viewed on July 9, 2008).

15. James Lyons, *Selling Seattle: Representing Contemporary Urban America* (London: Wallflower, 2004), 120.

16. The decisive distance between grunge and riot grrrl is realized in the magnificent incoherence of Hole, one of the era's great bands not despite but because they tried to synthesize the fundamentally incommensurate desires of the two formations.

17. Legs McNeil and Gillian McCain, *Please Kill Me: The Uncensored Oral History of Punk* (New York: Grove Press, 1996), 173.

18. John Robb, "White Heat," *Sounds,* October 21, 1989.

19. Andrew Smith, "Sound and Fury," *Observer,* October 1, 2001.

20. For all the slinky, sinister magic of TLC's 1994 R&B hit "Creep," it would be hard to argue for it as a continuation of grunge by other means.

21. The mortified flesh of the crucified eremite in the video for "Heart Shaped Box" is the visual representation of this situation.

22. Rick Marin, "Grunge: A Success Story," *New York Times,* November 15, 1991, Style section.

23. "Pearl's Jam," *Entertainment Weekly,* November 19, 1993.

24. The clearest account of this is in Gertrude Stein's ventriloquized verdict on Picasso: "Only that Picassos were rather awful and the others were not. Sure, she said, as Picasso once remarked, when you make a thing, it is so complicated making it that it is bound to be ugly, but those that do it after you they don't have

to worry about making it and they can make it pretty, and so everyone can like it when the others make it." Gertrude Stein, *The Autobiography of Alice B. Toklas* (New York: Random House, 1960), 23.

25. One notes in passing that the cover of *Nevermind* features a submerged baby, as does the video clip for "Come as You Are"; the suggestions of interiorization and submersion in the title of *In Utero* have already been mentioned.

26. Marcus, *In the Fascist Bathroom,* 370.

BRIDGE: Just a Stop Down the Line

1. Not that this was a new phenomenon; it was already dated by the moment John Lennon proclaimed the Beatles bigger than Jesus.

2. As exemplified by previous singles such as "Sunday Bloody Sunday," "Pride (in the Name of Love)," and "I Still Haven't Found What I'm Looking For."

3. Three of these hit number one on the Modern Rock chart; two hit number five; yet another hit number seven.

4. The album was recorded in part at the same studio, Hansa Ton, where David Bowie worked on *Low* and *Heroes,* a rather specific connection. However, the general matter is perhaps more worthy of consideration: there is likely an entire study to be written on drag in Berlin and its relation to pop music. The Weimar milieu glossed by *Cabaret* (stage musical 1966, film version 1972) provides suggestive ground for seeing Berlin as a long-standing locus of performance and passing (man/woman, gay/straight, Jew/Christian), which drag both exemplifies and allegorizes. However, the panic of the binaries reaches its apex with specific reference to the Berlin Wall in *Hedwig and the Angry Inch* (stage musical 1998, film version 2001). The opening number, "Tear Me Down" (words and music by Stephen Trask), begins with Hedwig (John Cameron Mitchell) demanding, "Don't you know me, Kansas City? I'm the new Berlin Wall!" The Wall serves as a vehicle for Hedwig to make an account of herself as forever *between:* to assess her career as a semiprofessional rock singer, and to narrate her incomplete M/F transition. A lengthy interlude spoken by a bandmate summarizes the history of the Wall, including the following:

> We thought the Wall would stand forever and now that it's gone we don't know who we are anymore. Ladies and Gentlemen, Hedwig is like that wall, standing before you in the divide between East and West, slavery and freedom, man and woman, top and bottom, and you can try and tear her down, but before you do, you must remember one thing . . .

—at which point Hedwig returns to pick up the vocal:

> Ain't much of a difference—between a bridge and a wall
> Without me right in the middle, babe, you would be nothing at all.

4. THE BILLBOARD CONSENSUS

1. There is no doubt that people often use the term *pop* in an attempt to denote a musical style, with inevitable ambiguity. The reference is often to certain conventions of melody and to one of the established variations of "American song form." For a long while it meant *in the tradition of the Beatles*. The best understanding bridges the economic and aesthetic, indicating genre songs that have smoothed their subcultural identifiers down to hooks that might catch listeners from other subcultures. Even this is not true of every pop song. Finally, they are married only by the marketplace.

2. Though not all; the puzzling history of which genres qualified—and when—for the Hot 100 is deserving of its own study as well. In some cases, genres that had their own charts, such as Country, seemed excluded from the pop charts; in others, such as Hot Black Singles (1982–1990), this was manifestly not the case.

3. Jane Dark, "Fair Maidens," *Village Voice*, May 12, 1998, 118.

4. Surely a reference to the Madonna song discussed later in this chapter, and surrounding events (see p. 97).

5. Hsu, "Three Songs from the End of History," 12.

6. *Blender,* circa April 2004.

7. The politburo of the German Democratic Republic had planned to open the border on November 10; thanks to a historical miscommunication, the transit began a day early.

8. As part of its release, it premiered in a Pepsi commercial that would swiftly be pulled from the air because the song's actual video was deemed blasphemous—the referent, certainly, of Joel's "rock 'n' roller cola wars."

9. J. D. Considine, "Like a Prayer: Madonna's True Confessions," *Rolling Stone,* April 6, 1989, 79–80.

10. Pamela Robertson, *Guilty Pleasures: Feminist Camp from Mae West to Madonna* (Durham, N.C.: Duke University Press, 1996), 117.

11. World Party, *Goodbye Jumbo* (Papillon, 1990).

12. The inverse of O'Connor's solemnity would be Prince's gymnastic duet with Rosie Gaines, on *The Hits, The B-Sides* (Warner Bros., 1993).

13. Most famous for later shredding a photograph of Pope John Paul II on a national broadcast to protest child abuse, O'Connor began her public career with the Public Enemy logo shaved into her buzzcut.

14. Luce Irigaray, *This Sex Which Is Not One,* trans. Catherine Porter and Carolyn Burke (Ithaca: Cornell University Press, 1985), 24.

15. Also composed in 1990 and released in 1991, Cathy Dennis's "Too Many Walls" would reach number one on the Adult Contemporary charts. No, really.

16. EMI, 2004. The album also includes "My Sharona," by the Knack (five singles on the Hot 100 in the space of two years), and "Mary's Prayer" by Danny Wilson, encountered earlier.

17. "Dance Music Celebrates End of a Deee-Liteful Year," *Billboard,* December 22, 1990, 40.

18. Elektra, 1990.

19. Cf. p. 160, note 4, for a differing account of the bridge/wall relationship, which similarly holds in mind the levels of song structure, social relations, and (far more explicitly) recent history.

20. The only song that approached it, with twenty weeks on the chart, was called "Feels Good," by Tony! Toni! Tone! (Wing, 1990).

21. James Miller, *Flowers in the Dustbin: The Rise of Rock and Roll, 1947–1977* (New York: Simon & Schuster, 1999), 138–42.

22. Gina Serpe, "New Kids: Back on the Block?" *E!Online,* January 28, 2008, www.eonline.com/uberblog/b57329_New_Kids_Back_on_the_Block.html.

23. Needless to say, the scale of these numbers indicates that tweens and teens were not the only demographic purchasing the music.

24. Jon Pareles, "When Pop Becomes the Toy of Teenyboppers," *New York Times,* July 11, 1999, Arts and Leisure (section 2).

25. Gayle Wald, "I Want It That Way: Teenybopper Music and the Girling of Boy Bands," *Genders* 35 (2002), www.genders.org/g35/g35_wald.html.

26. Neil Strauss, "THE POP LIFE; Eminem Enters 'N Sync Turf," *New York Times,* June 7, 2000, Arts section.

27. "Teen & Tween Trends," *Datamonitor* (December 2004).

28. With the disappointing duration of Backstreet Boys' *Black & Blue* (Jive, 2000).

29. X-Ray Spex, *Germ Free Adolescents* (EMI, 1978).

30. EMI, 1995.

31. The technological changes include ever-more cost-effective storage and prevalent bandwidth capacity. As I have argued elsewhere, it is critical to understand the rise of file-sharing as a consequence of the history of the technologically expanded workplace and working day that comes into view with telecommuting and similar innovations. Digital file sharing, even as practiced by the idle rich and poor, is thus best understood as a sort of displaced and marginal retribution extracted by workers against the dynamic of ever-expanding labor time, finally more similar to taking home Post-Its from the office than to shoplifting. See Joshua Clover, *The Matrix* (London: British Film Institute, 2005), 72–74; and Piratebureau, "Supermovables: The Fate of Unreal Estate, or a Treatise on the Social Problem Regarding Illegal File-Sharing," *Other Voices* 3, no. 1 (May 2007), www.othervoices.org/3.1/pirate/index.php.

32. Increasingly during the nineties, "producer" comes to designate one or several of the roles of writer-composer, instrumentalist, arranger, DJ, sample designer, et cetera.

33. This is all that "tipping point" can really mean, despite its vogue as an intel-

lectualized marketing concept following Malcolm Gladwell's book of the same name (New York: Back Bay Books, 2000).

34. Obviously, the vinyl form of music staggered onward for more than a decade, in the guise of increasingly fetishized limited releases; 45 RPMs for juke-boxes before they completed their own digital conversion; and most notably in the guise of the 12″ single used by hip-hop and rave DJs. This last is compelling exactly insofar as it preserves the 12″ as a musical instrument rather than a simple storage device, observing, that is, the reproduction-as-production aesthetic that arose in a challenge to rock, in ironic counterpoint to the history of the vinyl record.

35. Fred Bronson, *The Billboard Book of Number 1 Hits: The Inside Story behind Every Number One Single on Billboard's Hot 100 from 1955 to the Present* (New York: Billboard Books, 2003), 745.

36. From the liner notes to the compilation disc *Don't Bore Us, Get to the Chorus!* (EMI, 1995).

37. "When I See You Smile," by Bad English: a song of such execrable vacuity that it offers the happy reminder that some songs really are better than others.

38. Raymond Roussel, *Selections from Certain of His Books,* trans. Antony Melville (London: Serpent's Tail, 1991), 62.

39. Ildiko Vasary, "Comrades, It's Over!: The Election Campaign in Hungary 1990," *Anthropology Today* 7, no. 4 (August 1991): 6.

5. THE IMAGE-EVENT AND THE BLIND SPOT

1. They did not do so officially at least. The movies did it for them: first in 1948, the year of the Blockade, with Roberto Rossellini's *Germany Year Zero;* and again in 1991, when Jean-Luc Godard released the elaborately titled telefilm, *Allemagne année 90 neuf zéro* (Germany Year 90 Nine Zero).

2. Brian Massumi, "Navigating Movements," in *Hope: New Philosophies for Change,* ed. Mary Zournazi (New York: Routledge, 2002), 224.

3. James Joyce, *Ulysses* (New York: Vintage Books, 1990), 34.

4. Guy Debord, *The Society of the Spectacle,* trans. Donald Nicholson-Smith (New York: Zone, 1994), 49 [thesis 76].

5. "Everyone was there: the Red Army, journalists, musicians from Germany, from America, from Russia—the whole world on one boat. It was like a vision; everyone was talking the same language. It was a very positive vibe. That night was the basic inspiration for 'Wind of Change'" (interview with Klaus Meine, *New Music Express,* quoted in Songfacts, www.songfacts.com/detail.php?id=2764).

6. The hallmark of this analysis is Joe Carducci, *Rock and the Pop Narcotic: Testament for the Electric Church* (Centennial, Wyo.: Redoubt Press, 2005).

7. Jacques Lacan famously defined "the Real" as "that which resists symbolization absolutely"; Jameson amends this by stating, "Nonetheless, it is not terribly

difficult to say what is meant by the Real in Lacan. It is simply History itself" (Jameson, "Imaginary and Symbolic in Lacan," in *Jameson Reader*, 106). Well to recall that the Jesus Jones single preceding "Right Here, Right Now" was titled "Real, Real, Real," as if Lacan's three registers of Real, Symbolic, and Imaginary had been overcome in an instant of absolute history. At least if one takes pop to be a meditation on theory as well as vice versa, which is a pleasing form of thought indeed.

8. The spot is titled "The Absolute," and was produced by TWBA/Chiat/Day, 2006.

9. Jacques Derrida, *Of Spirit: Heidegger and the Question*, trans. Geoffrey Bennington and Rachel Bowlby (Chicago: University of Chicago Press, 1991); *Specters of Marx: The State of the Debt, the Work of Mourning, and the New International* (New York: Routledge, 1994).

10. The song was written by James Myers and Max Freedman in late 1952, and originally recorded by Sonny Dae and His Knights; Haley, for whom it was intended, first released it in 1954 to limited notice. Pop, the art of the present, must always wait for the right present to heave into view. See Jim Dawson and Steve Propes, *What Was the First Rock 'n' Roll Record?* (London: Faber & Faber, 1992).

11. Greil Marcus, "Stories of a Bad Song," *Threepenny Review*, no. 104 (Winter 2006): 6.

12. Marcus, *In the Fascist Bathroom*, 383–84 (slightly corrected against recording of event).

13. Debord, *Society of the Spectacle*, 114 [thesis 158].

14. Charles Armstrong, "Contesting the Peninsula," *New Left Review* (May/June 2008), 116.

15. Fukuyama, *End of History and the Last Man*, 14.

16. Ibid., 312.

17. Pico Iyer, "The Unknown Rebel," *Time*, April 13, 1998, 192.

18. "Marx says, revolutions are the locomotives of world history. But perhaps it is really totally different. Perhaps revolutions are the grasp by the human race traveling in this train for the emergency brake" (Walter Benjamin, "Paralipomena to 'On the Concept of History,'" in *Selected Writings, Volume 4: 1938–1940*, trans. Edmund Jephcott et al., ed. Howard Eiland and Michael W. Jennings [Cambridge, Mass.: Harvard University Press, Belknap Press, 2003], 402).

19. Wang Hui, *China's New Order* (Cambridge: Harvard University Press, 2006), 63.

20. Giorgio Agamben, *The Coming Community*, trans. Michael Hardt (Minneapolis: University of Minnesota Press, 1993), 85.

21. Against this, it becomes almost impossible to recall that the students repeatedly sang "The Internationale" while arriving and occupying the square, according to Amnesty International, *People's Republic of China: Preliminary Findings on*

Killings of Unarmed Civilians, Arbitrary Arrests, and Summary Executions since 3 June 1989 (London: Amnesty International, 1989), 19.

22. Wang, *China's New Order*, 181.

23. Gopal Balakrishnan, *Antagonistics: Capitalism and Power in an Age of War* (London: Verso, 2008), vii–viii.

24. Carl Schmitt, *The Concept of the Political*, trans. George Schwab (Chicago: University of Chicago Press, 1996), 88, 83.

25. Ibid., 90.

26. Balakrishnan, *Antagonistics*, viii.

27. Alain Badiou, *The Century* (Cambridge: Polity, 2007), 20.

28. Schmitt, *Concept of the Political*, 22.

29. Note in particular Detroit techno's much-bruited relation to twelve-tone music (beloved by Adorno), itself premised on the deployment of the scale without emphasis on any given note—effectively an antihierarchical rhetoric.

30. Sigmund Freud, *The Interpretation of Dreams* (Ware, Hertfordshire: Wordsworth Editions, 1997), 166.

31. Badiou, *Century*, 59.

32. This is Walter Benjamin's well-known description of "capitalism as religion," in the essay of the same name, *Selected Writings*, vol. 1 (Cambridge, Mass.: Harvard University Press, Belknap Press, 2003), 288.

33. Jameson, "Postmodernism," 203.

34. Jon Pareles, "When Pop Becomes the Toy of Teenyboppers," *New York Times*, July 11, 1999, Arts and Leisure, section 2, 32.

35. Garratt, *Adventures in Wonderland*, 165.

36. Dick Hebdige, "Un-Imagining Utopia," in *Sound Unbound*, ed. Paul Miller (Cambridge: MIT Press, 2008), 86.

37. In light of this, it is of some note that 1989 saw the publication of Allan Bloom's *The Closing of the American Mind* (New York: Simon & Schuster, 1987), a book of considerable reputation, not the least because its author was a leading cultural figure of the neoconservative movement that worked so admirably for all that closure.

38. Jameson, *Political Unconscious*, 76.

39. Jameson, *Singular Modernity*, 193.

40. Immanuel Wallerstein, *After Liberalism* (New York: New Press, 1995), 1, 3. Wallerstein's certitude about the fate of Marxism-Leninism seems, as of 2009, perhaps premature; certainly its specter keeps rising from the debris of global economic collapse.

41. This concept obviously draws on that of the "vanishing mediator," popularized by Žižek in *For They Know Not What They Do: Enjoyment as a Political Factor* (London: Verso, 2002), though earlier articulated by Jameson in "The Vanishing Mediator, or, Max Weber as Storyteller" (1973), in *The Ideologies of Theory* (London: Routledge, 1988), 3–24.

EPILOGUE

1. The logic of this alliance includes within it such events as Berlin's hosting of the FIFA World Cup in 2006, a fearsome generator of building activity.

2. Benjamin, *Arcades Project,* L1,3.

3. Another exception, albeit only on paper, is the work of the architect Lebbeus Woods, who in 1990–1991 designed a series of emendations to the city of Berlin, "Drawings for the Berlin Free-Zone," often involving mysterious forms lodged inside preexistent buildings (especially within dull gray apartment towers redolent of Eastern Bloc housing). Seen in cutaway views, they provide the sense of an impacted and alien life densifying the city center, entirely and presciently opposite to the machined and technocratic transparency that would shortly come to dominate downtown. Some of the images can be found in Lebbeus Woods, *Experimental Architecture* (New York: D.A.P., 2004).

works cited

Adorno, Theodor. *Aesthetic Theory*. Minneapolis: University of Minnesota Press, 1997.

———. "On Popular Music." In *Cultural Theory and Popular Culture*, ed. John Storey, 197–98. Athens: University of Georgia Press, 1998.

Agamben, Giorgio. *The Coming Community*. Trans. Michael Hardt. Minneapolis: University of Minnesota Press, 1993.

Altman, Rick. *The American Film Musical*. Bloomington: Indiana University Press, 1987.

Amnesty International. *People's Republic of China: Preliminary Findings on Killings of Unarmed Civilians, Arbitrary Arrests, and Summary Executions since 3 June 1989*. London: Amnesty International, 1989.

"Anthony H. Wilson: Excerpts from the Interview with Eyewitness in Manchester 30 April." *Eyewitness,* April 30, 1998.

Armstrong, Charles. "Contesting the Peninsula." *New Left Review,* May–June 2008, 116.

Badiou, Alain. *The Century*. Cambridge: Polity, 2007.

Bainbridge, Luke. "A Second Summer of Love." *Observer,* April 20, 2008, 46.

Balakrishnan, Gopal. *Antagonistics: Capitalism and Power in an Age of War*. London: Verso, 2008.

Benjamin, Walter. *The Arcades Project*. Trans. Howard Eiland and Kevin McLaughlin. Cambridge, Mass.: Harvard University Press, Belknap Press, 1999.

———. *Selected Writings, Volume 4: 1938–1940*. Ed. Howard Eiland and Michael W. Jennings. Cambridge, Mass.: Harvard University Press, Belknap Press, 2003.

"Biology Raves." *Fantazia Rave Archive,* July 17, 2008. www.fantazia.org.uk/Scene/orgs/biology.htm.

Bloom, Allan. *The Closing of the American Mind.* New York: Simon & Schuster, 1987.

Bolton, John R. "The Prudent Irishman: Edmund Burke's Realism." *National Interest* 50 (1997–98): 67.

Bronson, Fred. *The Billboard Book of Number One Hits: The Inside Story behind Every Number One Single on Billboard's Hot 100 from 1955 to the Present.* New York: Billboard Books, 2003.

Bruno, Franklin. *Elvis Costello's Armed Forces.* New York: Continuum, 2007.

Buchanan, Pat. "Speech to the Republican National Convention on August 17, 1992." *Patrick J. Buchanan: Right from the Beginning.* www.buchanan.org/pa-92-0817-rnc.html.

Burke, Edmund. *Reflections on the Revolution in France.* New Haven: Yale University Press, 2003.

"Capital Gold Announcement." *Billboard,* October 18, 1988, 64.

Carducci, Joe. *Rock and the Pop Narcotic: Testament for the Electric Church.* Centennial, Wyo.: Redoubt Press, 2005.

Cauty, Jimmy, and Bill Drummond. *The Manual (How to Have a Number One the Easy Way).* United Kingdom: KLF Publishing, 1988.

Chang, Jeff. *Can't Stop Won't Stop: A History of the Hip-Hop Generation.* New York: St. Martin's Press, 2005.

Christgau, Robert. "Capsule Review." *Playboy,* February 1989, 16.

———. "Jesus, Jews, and the Jackass Theory." *Village Voice,* January 16, 1990, 86.

———. "The Shit Storm." *LA Weekly,* 1989, www.robertchristgau.com/xg/music/pe-law.php.

Clover, Joshua. *The Matrix.* London: British Film Institute, 2005.

Collin, Matthew, and John Godfrey. *Altered State, Updated Edition: The Story of Ecstasy Culture and Acid House.* London: Serpent's Tail, 1998.

Collins, Patricia Hill. "It's All in the Family: Intersections of Gender, Race, and Nation." In *Decentering the Center: Philosophy for a Multicultural, Postcolonial, and Feminist World,* ed. Uma Narayan and Sandra Harding, 156–76. Bloomington: Indiana University Press, 2000.

Considine, J. D. "Like a Prayer: Madonna's True Confessions." *Rolling Stone,* April 6, 1989, 79–80.

Cross, Charles R. *Heavier than Heaven.* New York: Hyperion, 2001.

"Dance Music and New Music." *Billboard,* July 23, 1988, supplement.

"Dance Music Celebrates End of a Deee-Liteful Year." *Billboard,* December 22, 1990, 40.

Dark, Jane. "Fair Maidens." *Village Voice,* May 12, 1998, 118.

Davis, Mike. *City of Quartz: Excavating the Future in Los Angeles.* London: Verso, 1990.

———. "Uprising and Repression in L.A." (interview with CovertAction Information Bulletin). In *Reading Rodney King / Reading Urban Uprising,* ed. Robert Gooding-Williams, 142–43. New York: Routledge, 1993.

Dawson, Jim, and Steve Propes. *What Was the First Rock 'n' Roll Record?* London: Faber & Faber, 1992.

"De La Speaks." Interview, August 16, 2008. www.youtube.com/watch?v = Qx8t AD84zOo.

Debord, Guy. *The Society of the Spectacle.* Trans. Donald Nicholson-Smith. New York: Zone, 1994.

Deflem, Mathieu. "Rap, Rock, and Censorship: Popular Culture and the Technologies of Justice." Paper presented at the annual meeting of the Law and Society Association, Chicago, May 27–30, 1993.

Derrida, Jacques. *Of Spirit: Heidegger and the Question.* Trans. Geoffrey Bennington and Rachel Bowlby. Chicago: University of Chicago Press, 1991.

———. *Specters of Marx: The State of the Debt, the Work of Mourning, and the New International.* Trans. Peggy Kamuf. New York: Routledge, 1994.

Duncombe, Stephen, ed. *A Cultural Resistance Reader.* London: Verso, 2002.

Eshun, Kodwo. *More Brilliant than the Sun: Adventures in Sonic Fiction.* London: Quartet, 1998.

Freud, Sigmund. *The Interpretation of Dreams.* Ware, Hertfordshire: Wordsworth Editions, 1997.

Fritz, Jimi. *Rave Culture: An Insider's Overview.* Escada, Ore.: Smallfry Publishing, 1999.

Fukuyama, Francis. "The End of History?" *National Interest* 16 (1989): 3–18.

———. *The End of History and the Last Man.* New York: Free Press, 1992.

Garratt, Sheryl. *Adventures in Wonderland.* London: Headline Books, 1998.

Gladwell, Malcolm. *The Tipping Point: How Little Things Can Make a Big Difference.* New York: Back Bay Books, 2000.

Goodwin, Andrew. *Dancing in the Distraction Factory.* Minneapolis: University of Minnesota Press, 1992.

Hebdige, Dick. "Un-Imagining Utopia." In *Sound Unbound,* ed. Paul Miller, 83–89. Cambridge: MIT Press, 2008.

Hegel, Georg Wilhelm Friedrich. *Phenomenology of Spirit.* Trans. A. V. Miller. Oxford: Oxford University Press, 1979.

Hsu, Hua. "Three Songs from the End of History." *Believer* 3, no. 5 (2005): 12.

Humphrey, Clark. *Loser: The Real Seattle Music Story.* New York: Harry N. Abrams, 1999.

Irigaray, Luce. *This Sex Which Is Not One.* Trans. Catherine Porter and Carolyn Burke. Ithaca: Cornell University Press, 1985.

Iyer, Pico. "The Unknown Rebel." *Time,* April 13, 1998, 192–97.

Jameson, Fredric. *The Jameson Reader.* Ed. Michael Hardt and Kathi Weeks. New York: Blackwell, 2000.

———. *The Political Unconscious.* Ithaca: Cornell University Press, 1981.

———. *A Singular Modernity.* London: Verso, 2002.

———. "The Vanishing Mediator, or, Max Weber as Storyteller." In *The Ideologies of Theory,* 3–24. London: Routledge, 1988.

———. "What's Left of Theory." Paper presented at "End of Theory" conference, sponsored by *Critical Inquiry,* University of Chicago, March 7, 2002.

Joyce, James. *Ulysses.* New York: Vintage Books, 1990.

Klein, Naomi. *The Shock Doctrine: The Rise of Disaster Capitalism.* New York: Metropolitan Books, 2007.

Kojève, Alexandre. *Introduction to the Reading of Hegel: Lectures on the Phenomenology of Spirit.* Ed. Allan Bloom, trans. James H. Nichols. Ithaca: Cornell University Press, 1980.

Kokoreff, Michel, and Patrick Mignon. *La production d'un problème social: drogues et conduites d'excès. La France et l'Angleterre face aux usagers d'ecstasy et de cannabis.* Paris: DGLDT/Ministère de l'Enseignement Supérieur et de la Recherche, 1994.

Lacan, Jacques. *The Four Fundamental Concepts of Psychoanalysis.* Ed. Jacques-Alain Miller, trans. Alan Sheridan. New York: Norton, 1978.

LaHoz, Sam. "Poli-tricks and Pimpin'" (interview with Ice-T [Tracey Marrow]). *Ugly Planet* 3 (2007): 39–41.

"Leader of the F.A.C." *New Music Express,* May 31, 1986.

Leigh, Danny. "Chillin' with Cube." *Guardian,* February 25, 2000, Friday Reviews section.

Lyons, James. *Selling Seattle: Representing Contemporary Urban America.* London: Wallflower, 2004.

Malausséna, Katia. "Commemoration as Staging Citizenship: The Example of the Bicentennial of the French Revolution." Paris: Université Paris 13/Maison française d'Oxford, 2000. www.univ-paris13.fr/CRIDAF/TEXTES/KMlpl.rtf.

Marcus, Greil. *In the Fascist Bathroom.* Cambridge, Mass.: Harvard University Press, 1999.

———. *Lipstick Traces.* Cambridge, Mass.: Harvard University Press, 1990.

———. "Stories of a Bad Song." *Threepenny Review,* no. 104 (Winter 2006): 6–7.

Marin, Rick. "Grunge: A Success Story." *New York Times,* November 15, 1991, Style section.

Marx, Karl. *Capital.* Vol. 1. New York: Penguin Classics, 1992.

Maslin, Janet. "Successful in Seattle: Turning Grunge to Gold." *New York Times,* November 8, 1996, Movies section.

Massumi, Brian. "Navigating Movements." In *Hope: New Philosophies for Change,* ed. Mary Zournazi, 210–32. New York: Routledge, 2002.

McLeod, Kembrew. "How Copyright Law Changed Hip-Hop: An Interview with Public Enemy's Chuck D and Hank Shocklee." *Stay Free!* 20 (2002): 22.

McNeil, Legs, and Gillian McCain. *Please Kill Me: The Uncensored Oral History of Punk.* New York: Grove, 1996.

Media Traffic. *United World Chart: The Official Global Hitlist.* September 1, 2008. www.mediatraffic.de/alltime-album-chart.htm.

Miller, James. *Flowers in the Dustbin: The Rise of Rock and Roll, 1947–1977.* New York: Simon & Schuster, 1999.

Mitterrand, François. "Press Conference on the Conclusion of the Fifteenth Summit of Industrialized Countries," July 16, 1989. www.g7.utoronto.ca/sum mit/1989paris/press_english.html (G8 Research Group at the University of Toronto; accessed June 28, 2008).

Mohaiemem, Naeem. "Fear of a Muslim Planet: Hip-Hop's Hidden History." In *Sound Unbound,* ed. Paul Miller, 313–35. Cambridge: MIT Press, 2008.

Moore, Mark. "We Called It Aciiiiiieeeed." *Guardian,* April 20, 2008. http://blogs.guardian.co.uk/observermusic/2008/04/we_call_it_aciiiiiieeeed_contd.html.

Nichols, D.E. "Differences between the Mechanism of Action of MDMA, MBDB, and the Classic Hallucinogens. Identification of a New Therapeutic Class: Entactogens." *Journal of Psychoactive Drugs,* 18, no. 4 (1986): 305–13.

Pareles, Jon. "Public Enemy Rap Group Reorganizes after Anti-Semitic Comments." *New York Times,* August 11, 1989, Arts and Leisure section.

———. "When Pop Becomes the Toy of Teenyboppers." *New York Times,* July 11, 1999, Arts and Leisure, sec. 2.

"Pazz 'n' Jop Critics Poll." *Village Voice,* February 27, 1990.

"Pearl's Jam." *Entertainment Weekly,* November 19, 1993.

Perse, Saint-John. *Anabasis.* Trans. T.S. Eliot. New York: Harcourt, Brace, 1949.

Piratebureau. "Supermovables: The Fate of Unreal Estate, or a Treatise on the Social Problem Regarding Illegal File-Sharing." *Other Voices* 3, no. 1 (2007). www.othervoices.org/3.1/pirate/index.php.

"Public Enemy Ousts Member over Remarks," *Billboard,* July 1, 1989, 1.

Redhead, Steve, ed. *Rave Off: Politics and Deviance in Contemporary Youth Culture.* Brookfield, Vt.: Avebury, 1993.

Retort (Boal, Iain, et al.). *Afflicted Powers: Capital and Spectacle in a New Age of War.* London: Verso, 2005.

Reynolds, Simon. *Energy Flash: A Journey Through Rave Music and Dance Culture.* Lodon: Picador, 1998.

———. *Generation Ecstasy: Into the World of Techno and Rave Culture.* Boston: Little, Brown, 1998.

Robb, John. "White Heat." *Sounds,* October 21, 1989.

Robertson, Pamela. *Guilty Pleasures: Feminist Camp from Mae West to Madonna.* Durham, N.C.: Duke University Press, 1996.

Rose, Tricia. *Black Noise.* Hanover, N.H.: Wesleyan University Press, 1994.

Roussel, Raymond. *Selections from Certain of His Books.* Trans. Antony Melville. London: Serpent's Tail, 1991.

Saunders, Nicholas, and Rick Doblin. *Ecstasy: Dance, Trance, and Transformation.* Philadelphia: Quick American Publishing Company, 1996.

Savage, Jon. *England's Dreaming.* London: Faber & Faber, 1991.

———. "Machine Soul: A History of Techno." *Village Voice,* summer 1993, Rock 'n' Roll Quarterly insert.

Schmitt, Carl. *The Concept of the Political.* Trans. George Schwab. Chicago: University of Chicago Press, 1996.

Serpe, Gina. "New Kids: Back on the Block?" *E!Online,* January 28, 2008. www.eonline.com/uberblog/b57329_new_kids_back_on_block.html.

Shapiro, Peter, ed. *Modulations: A History of Electronic Music—Throbbing Words on Sound.* New York: Caipirinha, 2000.

Sherlock, Kellie, and Mark Conner. "Patterns of Ecstasy Use amongst Club-Goers on the UK 'Dance Scene.'" *International Journal of Drug Policy* 10, no. 2 (1999): 117–29.

Smith, Andrew. "Sound and Fury." *Observer,* October 1, 2001.

Stein, Gertrude. *The Autobiography of Alice B. Toklas.* New York: Random House, 1960.

Stoppard, Tom. *Rock 'n' Roll.* New York: Grove, 2007.

Strauss, Neil. "THE POP LIFE; Eminem Enters 'N Sync Turf." *New York Times,* June 7, 2000, Arts section.

"Teen & Tween Trends." *Datamonitor,* January 19, 2005.

Thomas-Glass, Dan. "The Dialectic of the Collective: Language Poetry Rap Music." Ph.D. diss., University of California, Davis, 2009.

United Kingdom. Ministry of Justice. The UK Statute Law Database. *Criminal Justice and Public Order Act 1994 (c. 33).* November 3, 1994. www.statutelaw.gov.uk/content.aspx?activeTextDocId = 2156203.

Vaidhyanathan, Siva. *Copyrights and Copywrongs: The Rise of Intellectual Property and How It Threatens Creativity.* New York: New York University Press, 2001.

Van Deburg, William L. *Hoodlums: Black Villains and Social Bandits in American Life.* Chicago: University of Chicago Press, 2004.

Vasary, Ildiko. "Comrades, It's Over!: The Election Campaign in Hungary 1990." *Anthropology Today* 7, no. 4 (1991): 6.

Virilio, Paul. *Speed and Politics.* Los Angeles: Semiotext(e), 2006.

Wald, Gayle. "I Want It That Way: Teenybopper Music and the Girling of Boy Bands." *Genders* 35 (2002). www.genders.org/g35/g35_wald.html.

Wallerstein, Immanuel. *After Liberalism.* New York: New Press, 1995.

Wang Hui. *China's New Order.* Cambridge, Mass.: Harvard University Press, 2006.

We Got Power Films. "David Markey's 1991 Tour Diary." August 18, 1991. www.wegotpowerfilms.com/archives/91_tour_diary.html.

Williams, Raymond. *Marxism and Literature*. London: Oxford University Press, 1977.

Wilson, David. "Constructing a 'Black-on-Black' Violence: The Conservative Discourse." *ACME: An International E-Journal for Critical Geographies* 1 (2002): 35–54.

———. *Inventing Black-on-Black Violence: Discourse, Space, and Representation*. Syracuse: Syracuse University Press, 2005.

Woods, Lebbeus. *Experimental Architecture*. New York: D.A.P., 2004.

Žižek, Slavoj. *For They Know Not What They Do: Enjoyment as a Political Factor*. London: Verso, 2002.

index

Page numbers in italic refer to illustrations.

antagonism, sociopolitical, 126–27, 136, 142; pop music's sublation of, 121, 131–32, 133, 136, 137, 138, 139, 140. *See also* confrontation, sociopolitical

anti-Semitism, 26, 34

Appetite for Destruction (Guns N' Roses), 75, 78

architecture, in Berlin. *See* Berlin, architecture in

Arm, Mark, 75, 82

As Nasty as They Wanna Be (2 Live Crew), 36

avant-rock, 75

Backstreet Boys, 102, 103

"Back to Life (However Do You Want Me)" (Soul II Soul), 67

Bad English, 163n37

Bakunin, Mikhail, 78

Balakrishnan, Gopal, 126

Balearic sound, 57, 63, 138

Bambaataa, Afrika, 28

Bastille, storming of, xi, xii

"Batterram" (Toddy Tee), 153n24

Beastie Boys, 14, 31, 34, 43, 51

The Beatles, 81, 92, 104, 133, 158n38, 160n1, 161n1

The Beatmasters, 67, 158n36

Belief (Nitzer Ebb), 71

belles époques: political, 5, 20, 119, 133; popcultural, 92, 93, 97, 106, 108, 118, 119, 133, 158n38

Beltram, Joey, 158n37

Benjamin, Walter, 142, 151n12, 164n18, 165n32

Bennett, William, 44

Berlin: architecture in, 141–45, *142, 144,* 166n3; drag culture in, 160n4; World Cup soccer finals in, 166n1

Berlin Wall, fall of. *See* Fall of the Wall

Betty Boo and the Beatmasters, 67

Bicentennial, French, xi

"Big Cheese" (Nirvana), 75

Bikini Kill, 80

Billboard (periodical), 42, 46, 66, 92, 101

Biology (rave promoter), 64–65

Biz Markie, 14, 41

Black Box, 67–68

black metal, 73

black-on-black violence, 37, 38, 44, 45, 47, 128, 139, 153n30

black-on-white violence, 45–46

Black Power/Black Nationalist rap, 25, 27, 30–41; and confrontational politics, 30–35, 128, 139; and conscious rap, 52; and Islam, 28–32, 44; and rhetoric of self-empowerment, 29–30; and transition to gangsta rap, 27–28, 34–41, 44, 52, 128

Black Power/Black Nationalist rap, artists associated with: Ice Cube, 40, 44; N.W.A., 27, 37, 39–41; Public Enemy, 25, 27, 30–35; Rakim, 29–30

Black Sabbath, 73

Bleach (Nirvana), 16, 75, 81, 82, 83

"Blew" (Nirvana), 81

blind spot, historical, 20, 136, 138, 143, 145

bling, 47, 49

Bloom, Allan, 165n37

Body Count (Body Count), 46

Bolton, John R., 150n3

Bomb Squad, 25, 32–33, 39, 40, 44, 48, 128, 136

Bomb the Bass (Tim Simenon), 43, 67, 156n17

Bon Jovi, 73

"Boredom" (The Buzzcocks), 77

boundlessness: of market relations, 120; in pop music, 95, 97, 105, 118, 120, 130

Bowie, David, 160n4

boy bands, 102–3

Boys Own (rave zine), 64

"Boyz N the Hood," 38, 40, 47

Bratmobile, 80

Brill, Dmitri, 101

"Bring the Noise" (Public Enemy), 31

Britpop, 56

Broadus, Cordozar Calvin, Jr. *See* Snoop Dog

Brown, James, 27, 56, 101, 155n46

Buchanan, Pat, 154n44

"Buffalo Stance" (Neneh Cherry), 42–43, 156n17

"Bullet the Blue Sky" (U2), 131

Burke, Edmund, 150n3

Burks, Jonathan, 49

Burning Man festival, 69

Happy Mondays, 15, 54, 56, 68, 116, 156n9
Harlo, Chilo, 65
Hart, David, 134
Havel, Václav, 5, 6, 108, *109*
Haywood, Leon, 48
"Heart Shaped Box" (Nirvana), 86, 159n21
Hebdige, Dick, 135
hedonism, in rave culture, 55, 56, 57, 131
Hedwig and the Angry Inch, 160n4
Hegel, G. W. F., 1, 115, 141, 149n2, 150n3
Hell, Richard, 80
"Here's Where the Story Ends" (The Sundays), 122
Heroes (David Bowie), 160n4
Heston, Charlton, 46
"Hey Now (Mean Muggin)" (Xzibit), 153n30
hip-hop. *See* rap/hip-hop
hippies, 16, 51, 55
history: blind spot in representations of, 136, 138, 143, 145; and difference, 87–88; end of, 1, 2, 8, 12, 18, 19, 20, 115, 117, 118, 120, 122, 126, 132, 143; identified with antagonism, 136; as pop, 109, 115, 135, 138; pop music's registration of, 2, 3, 4, 7, 8, 17–19, 20, 93–95, 109, 118, 127, 132, 135, 140; Real of, 8, 118, 121, 136
Hole, 159n16
Hot 100, 17, 18, 42, 92–93, 96, 98, 100, 106, 108, 124, 131, 139, 161nn2,16
Hothouse, 158n36
Houston, Whitney, 66
Hsu, Hua, 94, 150n4
"A Huge Ever Growing Pulsating Brain That Rules from the Centre of the Ultraworld (Loving You)" (The Orb), 60
Humanoid, 66–67
"The Humpty Dance" (Digital Underground), 14, 43–44
Hungary, post-Communist elections in, 108–9
hypervisibility, 116, 137, 138, 141, 143

Ibiza, dance music in, 55, 57
Ice Cube, 38, 40, 44, 46
Ice-T, 46, 153n24
ideologeme, Jamesonian, 135
ideology: and collapse of communism, 123, 124, 126, 137; and conservative critique of gangsta rap, 46; correlated with aesthetic form, 28, 29; end of, 8; and images of unification, 13, 144; of pop music, 8, 20, 100, 118, 136, 138; "postcompetitive," 100; of rave culture, 52, 56, 61, 63, 68, 72; of transparency, 142–45; and "war on terror," 21
"I'll House You" (Jungle Brothers), 52
image-event: Cold War as, 113–16; Fall of the Wall as, 11, 13, 18–20, 113–15, 116, 123, 137, 140, 141; and historical closure, 135; and historical groundlessness, 132; and hypervisibility, 116, 137, 138, 141, 143; and Jesus Jones's "Right Here, Right Now," 115–18
industrial genre, 71–72
Inner City, 67
internalization of struggle, in gangsta rap, 34, 37, 46, 47, 48, 128, 139
"The Internationale," xii, 164n21
In Utero (Nirvana), 86
inversion: and industrial genre's relation to acid house, 72; in rap/hip-hop, 31, 48
inward turn of grunge, 72, 80–89, 129–30, 131
Irigaray, Luce, 99
Islam: in rap/hip-hop, 21, 25, 28–32, 44, 49; and "war on terror," 21
"I Still Haven't Found What I'm Looking For" (U2), 160n2
"I Touch Myself" (Divinyls), 99
"It's the End of the World as We Know It (and I Feel Fine)" (R.E.M.), 93–94
It Takes a Nation of Millions to Hold Us Back (Public Enemy), 14, 25, 27, 31
"I Want'a Do Something Freaky to You" (Leon Haywood), 48

Jackson, George, 38
Jackson, Jonathan, 38
Jackson, Michael, 16, 83
Jackson, O'Shea. *See* Ice Cube
"Jack to the Sound of the Underground" (Hothouse), 158n36
Jacobs, Greg. *See* Shock G
Jacobs, Marc, 86
Jahn, Helmut, 143

Compositor:	BookMatters, Berkeley
Indexer:	Andrew Joron
Text:	11.25/13.5 Adobe Garamond
Display:	Berthold Akzidenz Grotesque
Printer/Binder:	Thomson-Shore, Inc.